REINVENTING COMMUNICATION

D1517082

Also available from ASQC Quality Press

Process Reengineering: The Key to Achieving Breakthrough Success
Lon Roberts

Team Fitness: A How-To Manual for Building a Winning Work Team
Meg Hartzler and Jane E. Henry, Ph.D.

Mapping Work Processes
Dianne Galloway

The ASQC Total Quality Management Series

  TQM: Leadership for the Quality Transformation
  Richard S. Johnson

  TQM: Management Processes for Quality Operations
  Richard S. Johnson

  TQM: The Mechanics of Quality Processes
  Richard S. Johnson and Lawrence E. Kazense

  TQM: Quality Training Practices
  Richard S. Johnson

To request a complimentary catalog of publications, call 800-248-1946.

REINVENTING COMMUNICATION

A Guide to Using Visual Language for Planning, Problem Solving, and Reengineering

Larry Raymond

ASQC Quality Press
Milwaukee, Wisconsin

REINVENTING COMMUNICATION: A GUIDE TO USING VISUAL LANGUAGE FOR PLANNING, PROBLEM SOLVING, AND REENGINEERING
Larry Raymond

Library of Congress Cataloging-in-Publication Data

Raymond, Larry
    Reinventing communication: a guide to using visual language for
planning, problem solving, and reengineering / Larry Raymond.
      p. cm.
    Includes bibliographical references and index.
    ISBN 0-87389-288-7
    1. Communication in management.   2. Communication in management—
Audio-visual aids.   3. Computer graphics.   4. Visual communication.
I. Title.
HD30.3.R39   1994
658.4'5—dc20   94-18254
                                             CIP

10 9 8 7 6 5 4 3 2 1

ISBN 0-87389-288-7

Acquisitions Editor: Susan Westergard
Project Editor: Kelly Cardinal
Production Editor: Annette Wall
Marketing Administrator: Mark Olson
Set in Galliard by Linda J. Shepherd.
Cover design by Paul Tobias.
Printed and bound by IPC Publishing Services.

ASQC Mission: To facilitate continuous improvement and increase customer satisfaction by identifying, communicating, and promoting the use of quality principles, concepts, and technologies; and thereby be recognized throughout the world as the leading authority on, and champion for, quality.

For a free copy of the ASQC Quality Press Publications Catalog, including ASQC membership information, call 800-248-1946.

Printed in the United States of America

   Printed on acid-free recycled paper

 ASQC
Quality Press
611 East Wisconsin Avenue
Milwaukee, Wisconsin 53202

This book is for Nancy,
who will remember for me.

CONTENTS

TABLE OF
VISUAL LANGUAGE
APPLICATION EXAMPLES

	Types of Benefits				
	Innovation	Cost Red.	Team Bldg.	Quality	
Examples by Functional Area					**Page**
Administration and Public Administration					
• Government downsizing and service improvement	x	x	x	x	112
• Public sector program planning	x		x	x	122
• Facilities management	x	x	x		120
Customer Service					
• Benchmark			x	x	90
Information Systems					
• Strategic planning	x	x			124
• Project planning		x	x		110
Organization					
• Restructuring	x	x	x	x	115
• Acquisition/merger	x	x	x	x	29

	Types of Benefits				
	Innovation	Cost Red.	Team Bldg.	Quality	**Page**
Sales and Marketing					
• Sales management strategy		x		x	3
• Sales process quality			x	x	17
• Merchandising	x		x		119
Supply Chain					
• Inventory reduction	x	x	x	x	109
• Transatlantic logistics	x	x	x	x	117
• Multicultural team	x	x	x	x	130

PREFACE

As you open this book for the first time, it is possible that you have never treated language as a variable in your environment, unless perhaps you have spent time overseas. Even then, you probably never considered the term *language* to represent anything other than verbal communication (in spite of the popularity of the term *body language*). Verbal language is one of our strongest paradigms.

This book is about visual language, a system of images used for communication and analysis. As you flip through the pages, you will see maps built with small images or icons. They seem playful and, at a quick glance, you could mistake them for a child's game. Why would you want to use them or even bother to find out about visual language?

First, visual language can extend your communication capabilities through a method that could be termed *iconographic mapping*, *thematic flowcharting*, or more simply, *picture stories*. These playful images have proven to be unexcelled as communication tools when the subject is both highly complex and emotionally charged. They've been used with great success in business, government, the military, and universities, but ironically, not yet in primary schools where playful appearance would be a natural attraction.

Second, visual language is a powerful creativity tool.

Third, using visual languages builds teamwork skills and is especially effective for multicultural groups.

I have applied a variety of visual languages during the past eight years, and this book is based on my personal experience and research. It describes actual examples and results accomplished in a number of companies and institutions. It shows how visual languages work and how to build new ones to suit a particular purpose.

Visual languages are different, but they certainly should not be dismissed as a gimmick of the 1990s. Images were used before letters were devised or words were written, starting with cave paintings and hieroglyphics. They are a natural way to communicate and their power originates in the eyesight, visual interpretation, and thinking methods that helped humans come to dominate other life forms.

A visual language can help you improve your personal effectiveness by

- Giving you the capability to use images and spatial relationships to take issues from the abstract to a more tangible, actionable form

- Accessing and applying your emotional resources and aligning them with your intellectual resources

- Increasing your creativity through greater fluency in the use of metaphors

- Helping you communicate more clearly

It can help you to improve your group's or process' effectiveness by

- Increasing group problem solving and direction setting capability

- Helping transform values into actions

- Increasing interworking skills and establishing an environment that encourages bonding

It can help you to renew your organization by

- Increasing the speed of participative decision making

- Increasing entrepreneurial spirit

- Establishing a new "rhythm" suited to participative leadership in lean, flat organizations

Most readers will learn about visual languages for the first time in this book, but they have been used without fanfare in one form or another in international service organizations for many years.[1] They have been applied in business in recent years with remarkable and consistent success in improving sales processes, reducing cost in supply chains, and improving customer service. No doubt, there are important new uses for visual languages in business, training, and education that have not yet been explored. I hope that this book will help you discover and realize them.

&ev; &ev;

I would like to thank and acknowledge the pioneering work of John Geesink, Bonnie Sontag, and Charles Revkin of Digital Equipment in visual language development and application to business problems. They were my teachers and much of my work was built on their symbol and process innovations.

I would also like to thank those who helped in improving the manuscript and documenting examples: George Dorros of the World Health Organization; Bill Woehr and Frank Smith of Hewlett-Packard; Bill Harvey and John Mrazik of Union Carbide; Barbara Chamberlain, Paul Meierhans, Graham Gleed, Gerry Wortham, and Jack Cotter of Du Pont; Coralie Bryant and Jerry Silverman of the World Bank; Andy Horsman of Neste; Peter Moyes of Digital Equipment; and Bruce Denner of the U.S. Air Force. Process consultant Ken Mayers provided valuable assistance in improving the manuscript and Pierre Jacot and his studio in Geneva, Switzerland, developed most of the drawings with support from Alex Raymond, Jason Bradbury, and Sean Raymond.

The map examples shown in the book were built using symbols developed at the Visual Language Research Center. To purchase color booklets of them, or for questions about building your own language that are not addressed in this book, contact

Visual Language Research Center
58 Salem Street
Andover, MA 01810
Telephone: 508-475-3045
Fax: 508-475-3478
Internet: 71732.1711@compuserve.com

INTRODUCTION

During the last few years, computer-generated graphics have shown that images not only are powerful tools to communicate information, but they are also excellent tools for analysis. Graphs, pie charts, and other images can reveal patterns in masses of historical data and forecast future trends. From strategic planning to process redesign and from the shop floor to the boardroom, images help with analysis, but they are seldom used for leadership tasks. Developing ideas, setting direction, and generating group commitment to objectives have stayed squarely in the traditional domain of spoken or written words.

Reliance on words in leadership tasks limits us to addressing complex, multifaceted, sometimes emotionally charged issues with a communication medium that is slow and prone to errors. Words arrive sequentially at the speed of the human voice. The receiver has to take in long strings of them and form mental images of what they mean. Those mental images are uniquely personal, not visible to others, and may not be what the sender intended. Mental images are difficult to verify with words. Left undetected, the misinterpretation of a word can lead to needless arguments, mistakes, and reduced efficiency.

This book is about visual language, a system of images that supplements words for communication and analysis. It shows how visual language helps people communicate on a deeper level, think more creatively, reconcile opposing ideas, and set common objectives. A visual language can define a vocabulary of symbols to represent functions, communications, problems, benefits, actions, obstacles, roles, and other matters of importance in organization life. The symbols are created in advance and used by people, most often in group settings, to build a visible image of a complex issue and resolve it. The language becomes a tool for participative group leadership.

Images present great quantities of information in parallel and at light speed. The information can cover the entire spectrum of possibilities from provable facts to assumptions, attitudes, and emotions. Visual languages make internal, personal images visible, stimulating discussion about them, improving understanding, and improving the probability of reconciling them with those of others. Because visual language represents ideas differently, people have to think about them differently and are more likely to generate creative insights.

The syntax and grammar for a visual language are provided by a metaphor that establishes a context for the symbols. For example, one visual language called *river mapping* uses a journey down a river to convey messages about strategies and plans. Its vocabulary of symbols represents the generic parts of a strategy such as actions, targets, measures, and responsibilities. A river represents the flow of time and symbols are placed alongside and on top of it.

Figure I.1 is a picture story about what you might do to create a visual language.

1. Your work requires sustained, coordinated effort, similar to rowing a boat.

2. Your first action is to foresee the requirements for symbols (using a telescope that sees into the future).

3. You then design the symbols.

4. The river forks, and you are faced with a choice of methods for drawing the symbols. You use a compass to decide which branch to take.

5. You may be attracted to the branch that has rapids because they promise speed.

6. Printing standard icons already available on computers would give you speed.

7. Unfortunately, this river branch has a waterfall. Your boat may not survive it because symbols built for other purposes will not work together harmoniously or appeal to users' emotions.

8. A lack of drawing skill blocks you from taking the other river branch.

9. You could undertake the hard work of carrying your boat around this obstacle by finding and working with a professional artist.

10. If you take this approach, it leads to an effective language and your efforts will be rewarded.

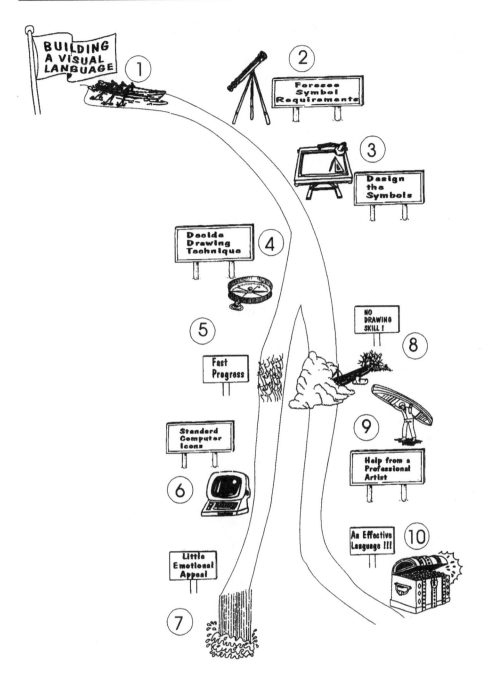

Figure I.1

This picture makes a mental map visual, stimulates discusion, and reduces the potential for misunderstanding. As you look at it, however, your first impression may be that it is childish. Such a reaction is not unusual. When adults first see a picture story, it reminds them of their childhood. As you read further, you will find that making you more childlike is one of the objectives of visual language because it is the child inside you that challenges limits and creates fresh ideas.

You may ask, "But why would I ever go to the trouble of learning or creating a visual language to tell such a simple story?" I suggest you probably wouldn't. You more likely would be interested only if you were challenged by a complex situation, the stakes were high, and you needed all the communication, creativity, and teamwork you could find.

An image stimulates your imagination but also helps ensure discipline in your thinking. For example, you may reflect about the telescope symbol near the beginning of the river and question, "How could I plan the symbols without first knowing just what I was trying to accomplish and who would use them?" If you were telling the story with the visual language, you would answer that question and add the appropriate explanatory symbols to your map. Colleagues working with you might ask other questions or make suggestions, and you would continue working on your map until it told the entire story. By requiring you to show all aspects of your strategy in a single image, your visual sense helps you judge its logic and completeness.

The visual language also helps you integrate your intellect and emotions. When you see the interconnections in an image and feel the emotions generated by the symbols at the same time, your logic and intuition complement each other and this synergy can make you clear and decisive. For example, if you believe that at some point you will face a serious risk, you might characterize it as a crocodile (see Figure I.2). This sends a message of danger: something could both upset the strategy and do harm to you personally! The crocodile symbol makes a

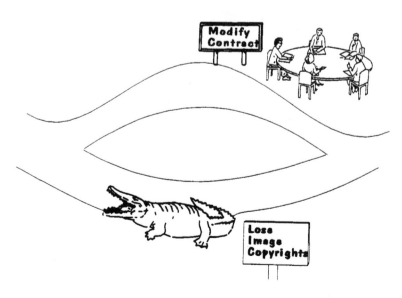

Figure I.2

strong statement about risk and, if you use it, you force yourself to show how you are going to avoid or deal with it.

Using a colorful, playful visual language can be fun, but it imposes discipline. When groups use a visual language to build maps, people discuss and negotiate the selection of each symbol. This ensures mutual understanding, increases precision, and guarantees group ownership of the completed image. When group members work intensely to solve an important issue, they develop interworking skills and bonds that facilitate future implementation.

This book will tell you more about how visual languages work, why they work, how to use them, and how to build them.

SECTION I

WHAT VISUAL LANGUAGES CAN ACCOMPLISH

CLARIFYING AND COMMUNICATING STRATEGIES

In September 1990, Bill Whitman felt out of control. Bill was a sales manager for an American electronics company. Based at the European headquarters, he was responsible for sales in 70 countries of varying size. He had been in sales nearly all his life. He could sell anything to anybody and had a proven record as a manager. The trouble was he had failed to meet his budget for the year. For the upcoming fiscal year, he had been able to negotiate a flat quota but he had gnawing feelings that once again he was going to come up short.

Bill needed a plan. Meeting his quota was the main thing on his mind but he knew that, to achieve it, he had to solidify his organization. There were a lot of factors to consider, and it was hard for him to think straight under the stress he was feeling. What could he do to turn things around? What would be the winning strategy? He needed clarity and simplicity so that he could focus his efforts.

On a Sunday afternoon, six weeks before the start of the new fiscal year, Bill sat down in his den and set out to build his strategy. He had an unusual tool with him. It was a booklet of colorful stickers that were the symbol vocabulary of a visual language called *river mapping*. There were about 15 pages of stickers that represented different actions and obstacles that could appear in the course of a project. They were colorful and amusing. A friend at another company had shown him how to use them to think out business problems a few months ago. The concept had struck him as kid's stuff then, not really a tool for engineers like himself, and he had put the stickers aside. But, this afternoon he needed something to help him bring his ideas together, so he was going to give the stickers a try. He laid the booklet and a flip chart–sized piece of green paper on his coffee table and sat down in his armchair.

He started to think about the things he wanted to do in the coming year, but his mind kept going back to old problems and then jumping to things he was doing now. To get these matters out of his mind and to discipline himself, he took out a spiral notebook and started listing some of the ghosts of the past and the issues plaguing him now. In about 10 minutes he stopped writing and decided to start using the stickers to show the past and present.

MAPPING A STRATEGY

The visual language required him to show how time flowed by using rivers and to show actions alongside the river. He first drew a sketch of a river flowing across and down the page. Then he took blue river stickers from the booklet and placed them on the green paper according to his sketch. He wrote the events and actions on signs and placed them along the river. Finally, he selected stickers that added some life to the signs he had written.

He showed how in 1986 the business was riding high, with 65 percent market share and the only worry was getting enough product to sell.

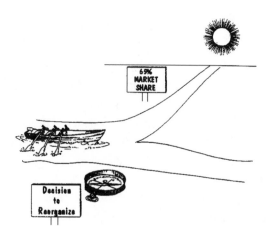

In 1987, corporate management had decided to reorganize and many good people left. Morale was low, sales were flat, and market share eroded.

In 1988 Bill was promoted from manager of the Middle East and northern Africa area to his present job. He set about rebuilding the organization and was able to exceed the European quota through enthusiastic leadership and personally helping conclude some big contracts.

He started a quality improvement program that, while only partly completed, led to improved customer satisfaction and decreased the costs per order.

He made quota in 1989 and, as the organization looked like it was regaining its vigor, he accepted an aggressive target for 1990.

The crumbling of the Communist Eastern block that year and the talk about reuniting Germany was exciting to read about in the newspapers but it was terrible for business and created problems that took all of Bill's attention. There was uncertainty across Europe but, in the critical West German market, sales stalled as companies waited to see what might happen and how their needs might change.

He was unable to recover those losses with sales elsewhere, and was not able to cut enough costs to compensate. As the sales engineers' morale slid, Bill reduced the quotas of some sales territories in order to keep them from becoming completely despirited. 1990 was lost, and prospects were not bright for 1991.

When he had finished telling this history with the stickers, Bill stood up and walked around the room. He liked looking at his map. It put him at ease to have shown all he had been through. He looked at the map again and decided to add a symbol to show how his colleagues' ambitions of building their revenue to a billion dollars worldwide by 1993 had to be buried.

So far, Bill's map looked like the one in Figure 1.1.

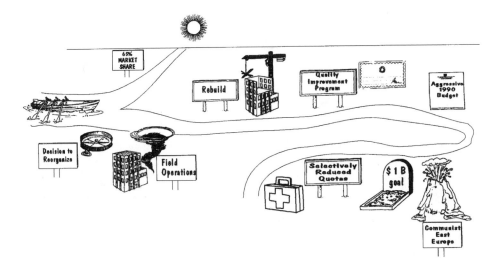

Figure 1.1

Having dealt with the past, Bill was ready to deal with the present. He wanted his map to show that the organization was starting fresh. Each country was currently wrapping up audits that recorded customer responses to a series of questions designed to capture their opinions of the quality of products, services, sales operations, and administration and to provide information about upcoming projects. These could be used as input for account planning and quality improvement efforts. Bill was creating an awareness of the need to recognize and break out of old ways of doing things and he was ready to introduce some new, flexible compensation incentives. These current activities are shown in Figure 1.2.

Figure 1.2

Mapping the past and present had been useful to clear his mind, but now Bill had to lay out his strategy, a much more difficult challenge. No light bulbs immediately flashed, so he started writing down all the actions that seemed logical. He finished without feeling that he had come up with anything inspiring and looked at the list to see if there were any natural groupings.

Two general categories started to show themselves. One was cost control and the other was improving selling performance, specifically, how to get each and every sales engineer to meet his or her quota. He decided that it made sense to designate them as his strategies for the year.

Bill put an *X* on the map to mark where he was now and focused his thinking on what to do to improve sales. His goal of getting each of his 350 sales engineers to make quota seemed an impossible dream, but it was unambiguous and motivating. He realized that clarity was the first thing that each sales engineer needed. Rather than face the new fiscal year with just high hopes and a vague idea of how to fulfill them, he wanted each sales engineer to have the clarity and confidence that a plan can provide. "The first thing the sales engineers should do," he said to himself, "is to make a forecast by customer. They can use the customer audit and their own knowledge of the customer base as the main inputs. From then on, it's just a matter of selling effectiveness." He represented the problem of an unclear strategy by placing a rock in the river and illustrated the forecast with a telescope.

Then Bill used additional stickers to help present his ideas. He thought about some of the early feedback from the customer audit where the sales function was criticized for not coordinating its efforts. Some customer accounts were not developed as fully or as effectively as they could have been because one salesperson didn't tell another about what she was doing. He characterized this situation as rapids in the river because there was the risk of losing control.

He decided to recommend that the country sales managers take it on themselves to help set up appropriate coordinating practices in their territories. He characterized them as a powerful elephant that could pull the salespeople out of a bad situation.

Bill looked at the list of actions he had made earlier. He guessed that he was paying dearly because he had not been able to convince his country sales managers that selling is a process that can be improved if measured and controlled at many points. They were convinced that "sales is an art," and resisted introducing any measures other than the dollar quota. Bill had dropped his efforts because of the political events and market problems of 1989, but now, after failing to meet quota, he knew he had to address two issues.

1. Sales engineers needed to understand the importance of spending more time face-to-face with customers. This he illustrated with a river branch going over a waterfall if too much time was spent in the office.

2. Sales engineers often spent a lot of time with customers they had known for years and liked personally, even though they had only small projects or no active projects at all. He showed this as a crocodile.

To reduce time spent on unproductive accounts and focus better on accounts with high-revenue potential, self-management tools, like those used in the Japanese subsidiary, would be effective. To show this, he depicted a river branch flowing past an oriental house that avoided the crocodile.

Bill also knew, of course, that competitors could disrupt any plans his salespeople could make. He decided that competitors were like pirates.

He decided that he should make himself more available to assist where a big win was crucial. He gave himself a paddle wheeler because he could use the power inherent in his position.

Bill noted all these points on signs, placed them along a river, and added visual symbols, as shown in Figure 1.3.

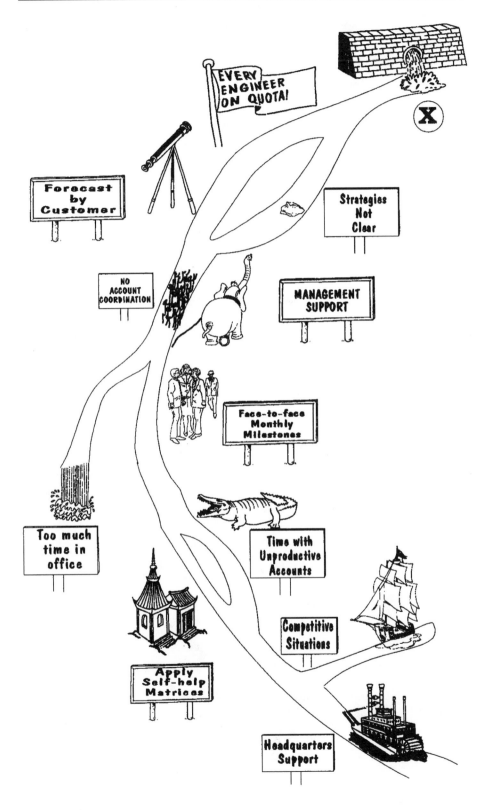

Figure 1.3

Turning his attention now to cost control, Bill wanted to show that many of the costs incurred by the country sales groups were for introducing new products and corporate programs. For small countries, like Greece and Portugal, sales volume could never recover the costs. He used a train to show the volume of programs delivered.

He picked a hippo to represent the costs of new products and programs because he saw the programs as big resource eaters that didn't intend to harm the boat, but could inadvertently sink it just by bumping into it.

After putting the sticker on the background paper, Bill realized he had to address this issue. He decided that each country would have to evaluate new programs and new products and select only a critical few to implement each year. He chose a scale to represent this action.

Bill then reflected about support processes like order entry, lead management, and literature distribution. Together they seemed like a beaver dam. They had been built by dedicated people, but they were slow and costly and blocked his cost reduction stream. Country sales managers tended to accept their inefficiency (and throw money into a swamp) because they had no desire to undo the work of a generation of support staff. Bill would have to take the lead and initiate efforts to get around them.

Bill decided that measuring performance in these areas and comparing each office against the others would spur improvements and make a significant impact on overall costs. He chose a ruler to represent this action.

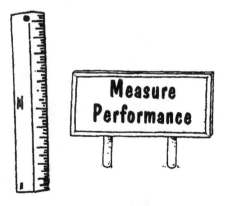

The cost control picture was now coming together (see Figure 1.4).

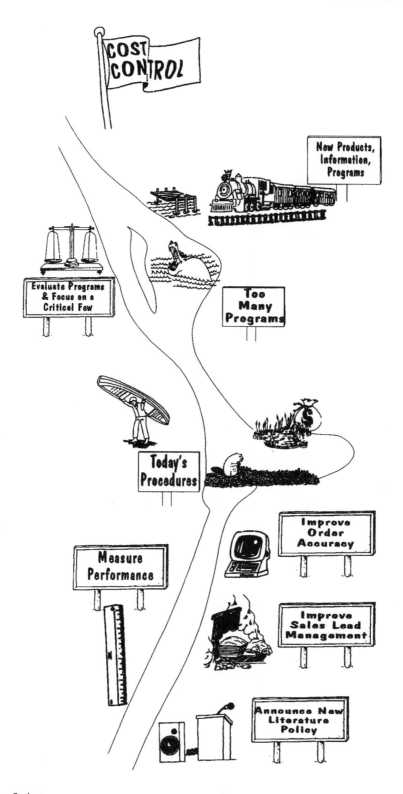

Figure 1.4

Bill knew that the sales managers might not like some of his ideas, but he was pleased to now have his thoughts in order and felt they made a forceful strategy. As he looked at the green sheet and colorful stickers on his coffee table, Bill noticed that something was missing: There was no sign of the customer at all. When he looked to see where customers could be represented, he realized that their interests should be behind nearly every action on the map. He selected the symbol of a pyramid to show that a timeless, overriding value behind his actions would be the needs of his end customers. Figure 1.5 shows the entire map, including the treasure island Bill believed was at the end of the journey.

Bill recovered his sense of being in control that afternoon and his confidence and determination started to soar. He had given faces to the shadowy bad feelings he had about the past and had declared what he would do in the coming year.

His individual action ideas, which hadn't felt very consequential or strong enough to deal with his problems, seemed to gain power when they were arranged into clear strategies. Now, he had a worthy plan!

Bill related what happened next: "Monday morning I got a call from my boss. He was on his way out of town on an unexpected trip and needed me to replace him and give a talk to the monthly meeting of all headquarters (HQ) employees in the cafeteria. The custom was that the vice president would review the state of the company and then another manager would talk about the direction of his or her individual business. Boy, was I glad that I had gotten my act together the day before! I sent my map out to be photographed and had an overhead transparency made.

"I titled my map *Rowing to Lake Success* and built my whole talk around it. The audience members really liked the symbols. That helped loosen them up so that my presentation became more like an interactive conversation than a speech. For example, many of the people present were responsible for delivering new products and programs to the countries. They said they liked being thought of as a train because they were proud of keeping to schedules. They asked if I thought they should provide more education or make other changes. I was impressed with the positive spirit they were showing but didn't want to get into a dialogue about it and suggested we take it up later with the managers in each country.

"The beaver dam got a lot of attention. One person said that, at his mother's farm, he uses dynamite to blow up beaver dams, but another said it wasn't right to hurt the beavers. I was worried this would get us off the point and into the ethics of managing a farm, so I broke in to say that the beaver itself was a positive symbol. Beavers work hard and can even change their environment by creating a pond. The problem in this

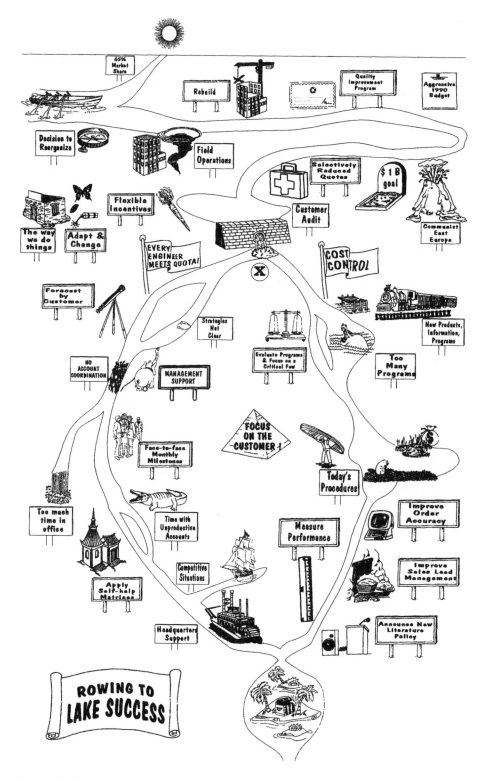

Figure 1.5

case was that all those little sticks had been put in place for reasons that belonged to a different era. Now they were an obstacle to our progress.

"Using the river metaphor and the symbols seemed to wire us all together. That big audience followed everything I was saying. Somebody made a joke about the elephant helping to save sales engineers from the rapids. She said, 'Can you tell me who the elephant represents? All our managers have about the same shape, and I can't see the face. Depending on who the elephant is, the engineers might be better off taking their chances in the water!' That got a good laugh, but it gave me the idea and the opening to say that the elephant represented the country sales managers, but that they didn't have any guidelines about account management either. I suggested that maybe one of the HQ staff groups could help by developing some.

"The discussion was fun and lasted about an hour. I felt good, not only about having developed a clear strategy, but also about getting everybody to understand it and want to support it. After the session, I received the best feedback ever. A clerk, for example, told me that my presentation was the first time he ever really understood any strategy presentation. Other colleagues were complimentary about my focusing on a critical few items and insisting on them. My peer from another division was impressed that I was able to get HQ people so interested in field operations. Now, all I had to do was deliver!

"I showed the plan to my boss the next day. He was very complimentary. He said, 'This shows the big picture very clearly, and what you plan to do makes a lot of sense. But, how are you going to get the country managers to get on board?' Then he asked, 'Why don't you get them to build their own maps?' That sounded good, since each manager needed to have a plan and needed to believe in it. It also gave me the idea that we might be able to make some sales process improvements at the same time."

SALES IMPROVEMENT PLAN

The following week, Bill held his monthly meeting with the sales managers and showed them the map. They liked the novelty of the map but were more interested in the ideas it showed, particularly the part about cost reduction in their countries. They also wanted to hear more about what Bill intended them to do to get every salesperson on quota. One grumbled that she thought his ideas about measuring and controlling face-to-face time had been discussed before and turned down because of too much paperwork. As a group, they told Bill they didn't think it was right to look at selling as though it were the same process in every country. Each sales manager felt he or she was different from the rest because of local market variations and different customs.

Bill said that, if every country used a different selling process, any improvements made by one could not easily be shared by others. Also, because he wanted to be more helpful on critical deals, he would have trouble communicating with sales engineers about where they were in the sales cycle. Then he asked the sales managers if they would agree to invest a few hours to review their selling processes with each other. He suggested that perhaps some of the unique steps they would identify might be adopted by the others. When the 14 agreed, Bill sent out for more visual language stickers. He broke the group into subgroups of three or four and asked the groups to build a map of how the sales process flowed in their countries, showing any variations they discovered. Bill also participated in one of the groups.

As the maps were being built, the members of each subgroup talked out how the process was conducted in their countries. They showed a single stream where they agreed and showed extra branches when there were differences. In about an hour and a half, the four maps were completed. One after the other, a representative presented his or her map to the full group. When all the presentations were complete, some differences were evident. The group that included the Middle East manager had shown how sales were made through distributors and other channels. One group showed detail about how pricing was established. Another went into more detail about generating sales leads. Still another showed points at which the process was measured and controlled by the manager. The images varied due to the interest of the group, but there was no disagreement about the core of the selling process.

The group was greatly surprised to find nearly total congruity of sales processes. They asked each other about anecdotes they had heard in the past about supposedly unique approaches, but found that the differences were only in language, emphasis, and folklore.

Bill said, "When we turned our words into pictures, we realized we all saw things the same way. It was like discovering a hidden asset! Right away, the Belgian manager suggested we consolidate the four maps into one, and the Spanish manager suggested that we spend some time defining measurements so that we could improve the process. That really made my day! This step was not exactly on the plan I had built that Sunday in my den, but it made a lot of sense and the whole group had a lot of ownership for it."

Because some of the managers had to catch early flights home, they nominated one person from each group to put together a consolidated map. The map is shown in Figure 1.6. With everyone's agreement, Bill wrote his four shorthand principles of successful selling on pyramids and placed them on the map. Key measures were written on an accompanying page, as shown in Figure 1.7.

The map starts in the upper left and shows that the sales process starts by filling a lake full of leads. A large stream contributes the sales engineer's knowledge of his own customer base, where an A,B,C analysis is performed and a plan is made for each customer. Market promotions and mailings also feed the lake. The sales engineer qualifies a lead by telephone and makes a trial close, an attempt to see if the product perfectly fits the need and if the customer is willing to make an immediate decision. If the trial close is successful and the customer says he or she will buy, a sale will likely follow with a minimum of risk and effort.

If the trial close is not successful, several meetings will be needed to define a solution and judge the fit between the product and need. There certainly will be obstacles, whether financial, technical, or a competitive offering. A great deal of effort is normally required, and the sales engineer continues as long as the customer gives favorable feedback.

The sales engineer's boat needs to stop to verify budget fit and technical fit and to talk to all the decision influencers to make certain that all the bases for decision are known and addressed. This should lead to a sale, but there is still a risk of losing control. If that happens, higher level management needs to become involved. Even after an apparent victory, competitors can offer surprise price reductions or free service and these have to be countered. If all the obstacles are dealt with, the order is taken, and installation is planned and implemented.

Bill recounted, "The most valuable thing about building this map was that it provided a common ground for those who believe selling is an art and those of us who view it more as a science. Everyone agreed that selling was like a trip into a jungle and that there could be some new surprise around every bend in the river. But, the managers could also see how measures could improve the process."

The next day Bill had the map photographed and sent it with copies of the narrative description to each member of his group. Within a few days he had received messages via electronic mail (e-mail) from a half dozen of them suggesting that all sales engineers be trained to use the map.

Bill liked the idea. It was customary to start the fiscal year with a meeting of all sales engineers and managers. "I thought, why not use this year's meeting as a training opportunity?" The map was integrated into this year's event.

"I started the meeting by reviewing our business goals and then explained my personal strategy using my map. It was just as effective as at my cafeteria talk. Later, we used the sales process map, talking it

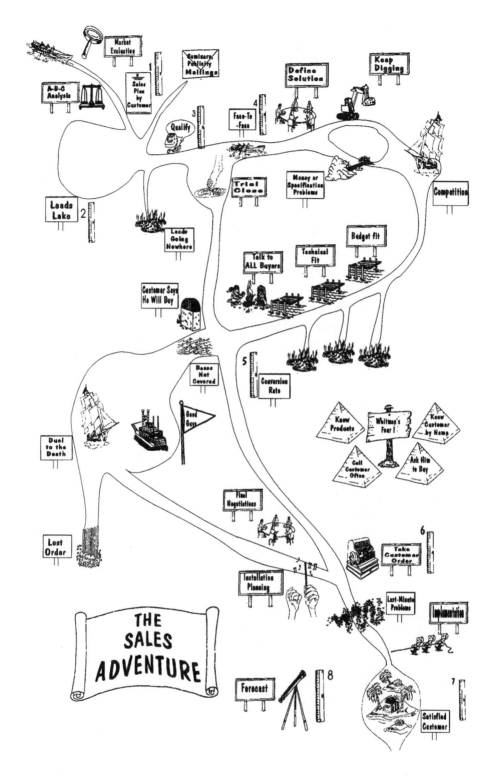

Figure 1.6

THE MISSION

CROSS THE PERILOUS SALES JUNGLE TO ACHIEVE FAME & FORTUNE. FOLLOW WHITMAN'S FOUR AND ARRIVE ALIVE!

A SUCCESSFUL MISSION

1. HAS A PLAN

2. SEEKS THE BEST ROUTE

3. CHECKS PROGRESS REGULARLY

4. AVOIDS DANGERS

5. OVERCOMES OBSTACLES

6. CALLS FOR HELP WHEN NEEDED

A SUCCESSFUL PIONEER HAS DISCIPLINE

1. SALES PLAN = CONTACT PLAN, CUSTOMER QUOTA
2. LEADS LAKE   =   3 X QUOTA
3. QUALIFIED LEAD = ONE BUYING INFLUENCER CONTACTED
4. FACE-TO-FACE = TIME IN FRONT OF CUSTOMER > 25 %
5. CONVERSION RATE = ORDER IN 50% OR LESS OF
                              NORMAL SELLING TIME
6. CUSTOMER ORDER = QUOTA
7. SATISFIED CUSTOMER = REPEAT BUSINESS, AUDIT
8. FORECAST = +/- 10% PER MONTH

Figure 1.7

through and introducing the new measures. Each of the sales managers participated in leading the session and pointing out different aspects of the map. We had lots of interaction and, by the end of the day, the 350 engineers were completely clear on where they were going and were highly motivated. After the session, some said they were ready for a new beginning and some said they liked the plan, but they all said they had a lot of fun.

"I'll spare you the alligator stories. We ended the year at 112 percent of sales quota and 5 percent under the cost budget. Market conditions didn't improve at all through the year, but we certainly did. We used that map constantly. It grew in power as the year went on. It was rich but simple and easy to communicate. The entire team could relate to the process and the measures.

"If you asked me what was the one key thing about this mapping exercise, I'd say that, because we were able to visualize the process, to really feel it, we were able to decide how to measure, control, and improve it.

"An analyst later looked at our map and made a traditional flow diagram out of it, just to see what it would look like. As you can see, it might be accurate, but it's work just to look at it and it sure doesn't get your blood moving." The diagram is shown in Figure 1.8.

This is the end of the example, but not the end of the story. Bill's organization also exceeded its objectives the following year. Bill and the managers later built another map, this time showing customers' purchasing process to better understand their actions and better meet their needs. At the time of this writing, they are still above quota.

Bill's example speaks for itself about how much can be accomplished while you have some fun at the same time. He and the group members clarified their thoughts by representing them visually and aligning them with their emotions. They achieved excellent communication with others because the visual language required them, as senders, to take the burden of communication onto themselves. They used symbols to give a face to their ideas. The symbols served as conversational lightning rods that connected sender and receiver. The river metaphor kept everything in context and made it easy to understand.

Chapter 2 shows an example of how a different visual language was used to solve a different kind of problem.

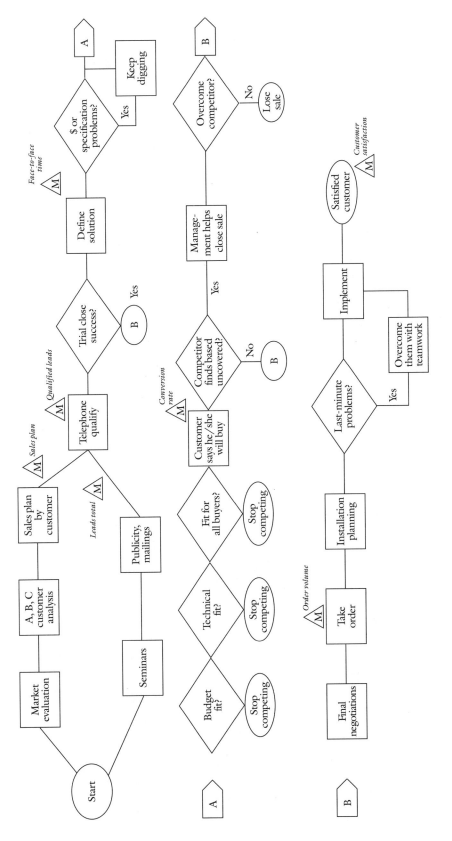

Figure 1.8

THINKING VISUALLY, REDESIGNING PROCESSES, AND BUILDING TEAMS

Being responsible for a group or project is similar to being a railroad engineer. Your locomotive is your project, product, or service. Your customers are on board your train. At some time in the course of your journey, you need to cross a ravine to reach your objective. A bridge, your human organization, straddles the ravine. Its three support timbers (communication, creativity, and commitment) will be all that stand between you and the rocks and water below.

A TRAIN CRASH

One engineer, named Matt Nelson, chaired the steering committee of a project to develop new maintenance systems for 10 manufacturing facilities. His company was enjoying favorable Wall Street reviews because it was downsizing and implementing a quality improvement program. Matt's project was a key part of that program and was forecast to yield major cost reductions during the next three years. His train was moving toward a ravine.

25

"I was determined to push as hard as needed to bring in the savings I had promised the board," said Matt. "Our new system had to be cus- tom-built because we were on the leading edge in this area. The other executives on the steering committee and I were happy that the infor- mation services director hired a top technical manager as project leader. We assigned well-respected people from the manufacturing, administra- tion, and finance functions, forming a strong team. The team was located at our Ohio River facility, but the software contractor we selected was in Denver. We put a liaison person in Denver to make sure every- thing stayed in sync.

"I got involved in this project because the stakes were so high. My main concern was to make sure that the benefits and return on invest- ment stayed on track. The project team members reported to us every month and their numbers were consistently good. They were always optimistic and had any data we wanted at their fingertips.

"The computer people led nearly all the discussions, but many of them were so technical that I couldn't follow them. They reported some schedule slippages and mentioned problems getting information from the contractor, but I knew that no systems project is ever smooth and thought that everything was in reasonable shape."

As the phase 1 installation deadline neared, there were signs that the contractor might not meet its schedule. When the deadline passed and only excuses were delivered, Matt hired a consulting company to audit the project. The auditors shocked him by reporting that missing the phase 1 delivery was only the tip of the iceberg. There had been a tremendous amount of rework due to misunderstandings and changed specifications. The project could be more than a year late and cost at least two times the original contract price. There was a high probability that it would never be completed because the contractor's resources and controls were in disarray and there was a risk of financial insolvency. The only good news was that a few of the key programs were finished and could be used.

"I was shocked and surprised and didn't know what to do or who to trust! First, I met with the project leader, the team, and some of the users. They thought the auditors were exaggerating the problems, and they wanted to send some of their people out to the contractor's site to help manage the system development and just trust that we could pull it out. I felt this was too risky and was concerned that we weren't on the same wavelength about the type of action that was needed.

"I had promised a big payback and we were already late. If we weren't going to deliver at all, the chair of the board would have to tell the Wall Street analysts about it. My meeting with the project team members had convinced me that they were too technical to see the business issues and didn't have the perspective to handle the decision, so I brought together a few of the steering committee members, our legal and financial officers, and the vice president (VP) of purchasing.

"We gathered data that confirmed the auditor's report and held a number of meetings. We talked about changing contractors, buying a software package, or taking over the development ourselves, but I didn't have enough facts to judge the feasibility of these alternatives myself. When I asked the project team members to investigate the alternatives, they quickly showed me that each had serious drawbacks.

"We searched for a long time but there was no way out. Fortunately, in reviewing our original cost/benefit analysis, I realized that the few programs that had been completed would give us a minimal payback. It wasn't my proudest moment but, after five months, we decided to cut our losses by stopping work with the contractor and salvaging the few completed programs.

"Changing gears to implement just the minimum, instead of the whole system, was quite traumatic for the team and took a few more months. First, the manufacturing users fought against accepting anything less than what we had originally planned, but they finally came around. Then, the project team had difficulty getting the programs running and reworking the business procedures. They finally wrapped things up, and I assure you, we're all happy that project is behind us."

In Matt's analysis, the problem was that the contractor didn't meet its obligations, thus leaving the company without alternatives. He was critical of the project leader for not effectively overseeing the contractor, yet he excused other problems as part of the normal background noise that comes with complex projects and relationships. An organizational change with new priorities shifted the company's focus, and Matt was able to move forward wtihout management questioning his actions and analysis.

An outside observer could argue that what really happened is Matt's bridge broke. The problem was that the project's human organization didn't work as a team. When faced with the contractor's failure, the communication timber (which was already weak) broke, and the creativity and commitment timbers followed. Matt's train crashed into the ravine because people from different backgrounds and perspectives did not perform together effectively when faced with a complicated and emotion-laden problem.

Matt didn't make the project team members full partners in the decision-making process because he had difficulty communicating with them and because he was afraid of the strength of their emotional drive to continue on the same course. As a result, critical knowledge and perspectives were left out and the promising ideas developed by his steering

committee could not be verified, refined, or built upon in the meeting. Because they felt disenfranchised, the team members put their energy into showing why ideas wouldn't work rather than finding ways to improve them. The lengthy process of exploring all possible ways to minimize the political damage shifted attention to peripheral aspects of the problem and away from its core.

Shutting down the project short of its goals is hardly the most imaginative solution Matt could have found, particularly given his company's aspirations. The fact that no better alternatives were generated was not because they didn't exist, but because Matt had not established an environment to facilitate creative thinking.

The time the team spent waiting for a direction to be set undermined its morale. When the decision was finally made, the team felt no ownership and was inefficient in implementing the new goals.

No communication, no creativity, and no commitment equals no results!

ANOTHER ENGINEER

A Swedish multinational company acquired a specialty, high-pressure plastic pipe company in England. Supplying it raw material from its own plastics plant, the Swedish company reasoned, would increase the profitability of both operations. The acquisition was formally made by its British subsidiary, which owned several other businesses including one that made a different kind of pipe. More savings were expected by coordinating marketing, material requirement planning, and administration in the subsidiary. Similar acquisitions had been accomplished many times before with excellent results, but it wasn't long before this one started to cause trouble. Janice Barclay was the purchasing manager for the specialty pipe company.

"While the negotiations were going on we were a bit nervous," she said. "Everybody acted professionally but the Swedes managing the takeover weren't very talkative. They were a bit distant. We understood that their culture was different from ours but it was hard to be comfortable around them. The day after the purchase we tested the Swedish raw material and wound up with faulty pipe. The Swedes said they had followed the specifications exactly and that any problem must be at our end. We, of course, replied that our quality had always been excellent with our other supplier's material, so it had to be their problem. The subsidiary's plastics experts got involved and we spent months performing analyses, testing and verifying everything imaginable. For all the big deal, the ending wasn't very dramatic. We found that there had just been a combination of small misunderstandings about the specifications for the material, so, we were both right and both wrong."

After all these troubles, when production shipments started, transport costs were higher than expected and delivery was not reliable.

- The pipe company's order quantities were too low to obtain favorable shipping container rates.

- Some material was contaminated during transit.

- There were shipping delays due to North Sea weather conditions, and the plant had to stop production for lack of raw material.

- The British subsidiary misentered a delivery date, which led to a late delivery and kindled fear of another production interruption.

- The trucking company that hauls the raw material from the port delivered more than the plant could off-load. This caused traffic hazards and a warning from local police that embarrassed the plant manager.

The pipe company's customers heard about these problems and the biggest customer was known to be looking for a new supplier.

"Everyone's nerves were getting raw, the level of trust was low, and frustration was high," continued Janice. "Problems in marketing added to the bad atmosphere. Our marketing people were increasingly at odds over objectives and tactics with the subsidiary, and relations had soured on nearly every level among the three companies.

"After a year, we were purchasing less than 20 percent of our raw material from Sweden. Customers were threatening to send their own quality control people to our plant, and the material we got from Sweden actually cost us more than our United Kingdom (U.K.) sources because the transport and related costs were so high. Nobody trusted anybody anymore."

Nobody wanted the merger to fail but that's what was happening. Clearly, Janice and the dozen other people with a major stake in the supply chain were either going to get it right or were going to get hurt. Janice thought about trying to meet the others individually and sort out the issues, but decided it would be slow and might raise political questions about her role and objectives. She also concluded that if they didn't develop an improvement plan all together, the ones not present would likely find fault with it and block progress.

Janice called for a quality partnership team to be formed with the objective of creating a more effective raw material supply chain and turning around the confrontational attitudes that had developed among the three companies. Management agreed with the need. Janice's 12 counterparts agreed to participate, but as she tried to organize a first meeting, everyone made it clear that he or she had other duties and not much time to invest.

Janice said, "Getting them together wasn't easy. I decided to ask for a two-day meeting, first because I didn't think the participants would agree to longer and second, I thought that if we couldn't solve the problem in two days, we never could. Our results were greater than we ever could have imagined. We designed a new supply chain that would have lower cost, fewer people, and greater reliability. By the end of the two days, you couldn't tell which company anyone worked for. We became that close!

"The plan and the good feeling were of course nice, but the real payoff was that within three months the changes were implemented! We're now using 80 percent Swedish material, which is our maximum because our contracts require us to have a second source. We haven't done all the accounting yet, but it looks like the supply chain costs are 35 percent lower than before. Our team stayed together and we've agreed to meet every few months to work out bugs."

This result is a dramatic contrast with Matt's computer system project. It provokes the questions How did Janice and her group do it? and Is it repeatable?

At first, Janice wasn't sure just what to do with the group and how to manage it, given the difficulties of language and culture and their diverse functions. The group included

Swedish Parent
- Logistics director
- Production engineer
- Pipe business manager
- Distribution manager
- Technical service engineer

British Subsidiary
- Customer service/order processing coordinator
- Product manager, pipe

Pipe Company
- Customer service manager
- Manufacturing supervisor
- Technology manager
- Product development supervisor
- Manufacturing specialist
- Purchasing manager

Janice decided that the starting point was to jointly understand how the supply chain functioned today, in detail. If the team members could agree on what worked well and what didn't, they would have a better chance of agreeing on what to do. She decided that the group should use a visual language called *village mapping*. On the first day she divided the group into four mixed subgroups and asked each to build a map showing the information and material flows.

MAP BUILDING

The map was built by taking paper symbols that had been made in advance and sticking them onto background paper.

Buildings represented business functions.

Envelopes represented information.

Roads represented the interconnection of functions and showed how information travels.

The groups started by talking about the situation and listing the component parts of the supply chain. The map building started when a woman selected a symbol to represent the Swedish plastics plant. She chose an older-looking factory because there was some resemblance. Another person wrote the company's name on a signpost and placed the sign next to the factory. Other team members added buildings and then envelopes and then roads. As they built the map, they reflected on it and talked it over, adding pieces until they had told the whole story.

When looking at the image they had created jointly, the team members studied each symbol in turn. They could see how the parts were connected, what worked well, where there were problems, and how serious they were. They tested the coherency and logic of the interconnections as they looked at them on the map. The individual pieces had to fit correctly with the overall map and they modified it until it looked and felt right.

The map builders were not conscious of their thought processes, but they were thinking visually.

- They used symbols and signs to represent the components of the situation and their spatial arrangement showed how the parts all fit together.

- Their choice of qualitative symbols showed the rough spots and faults in the process and evoked emotions.

- All the component parts, facts, and qualitative assessments were shown at the same time.

- Insights first appeared as intuition and were then supported by logic.

The team's map shows that orders for raw material are sent from the pipe plant to the subsidiary. The subsidiary retransmits the orders to the head office and works out delivery with the logistics function at the plastics plant. An invoice goes from the parent company to the subsidiary which then sends its own invoice to the pipe company. This flow parallels the formal organization of the total company.

As the team continued to work, it added more symbols to the map. Where the pipe manufacturing people saw a risk of a plant shutdown, they chose the symbol of fire to evoke the emotions of pain and urgency they had felt when it had happened the previous year.

People from the subsidiary selected the symbol of a mountain range to show that their distance from the plastics plant and Swedish parent presented formidable communication problems.

They showed their frustration over unappreciated paperwork through symbols of people walking in circles.

People at the Swedish plant didn't just talk about the extra inventory they kept to serve the pipe plant, they showed a warehouse sitting on top of a money bag.

Figure 2.1 is a simplified version of the overall map of how the supply chain worked at the time of the meeting. The facts of the situation could be seen and felt. By building a picture story with symbols, the team members came to understand and agree about the situation both intellectually and emotionally. They could see that operating the supply chain along the lines of the legal ownership structure brought about many inefficiencies. The more the group members looked at the images they had created, the more obvious it became that there must be ways to make the operation work better.

FLASHES OF CREATIVITY

The team members next turned to developing their ideas on how the supply chain could ideally operate. Figure 2.2 is a simplified image of the group's ideal supply chain map. The first idea for improvement burst out when the subsidiary order processing coordinator said, "I really don't see any reason why we have to be involved at all. We're just a truck stop for the orders and there's no reason why the two plants can't arrange the logistics themselves. That's what you do with your other suppliers." Following a silence, the subsidiary pipe product manager commented, "It would be a lot cleaner. Our businesses are different and we don't use the same kind of raw material anyhow. There's no advantage at all to our getting involved." He added, "Except that it means job security for the two of us!"

With the subsidiary removed from the picture, the group built a supply chain map where raw material orders would be directly placed to the plastics plant. After looking at the new map, the pipe manufacturing

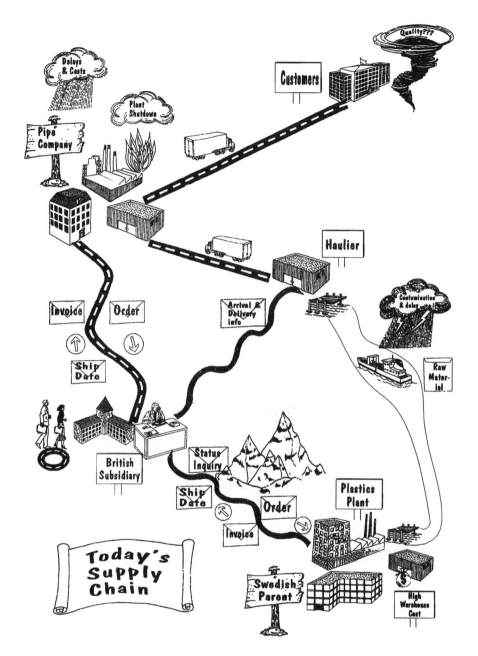

Figure 2.1

supervisor said, "You told us this morning that, to keep down freight costs from Sweden, you needed to plan bulk shipments. Since those are a big factor here, why don't *you* decide when it's best to ship? Instead of the pipe company sending you orders, we could connect you to our computer. You could see our customer demand forecast and our

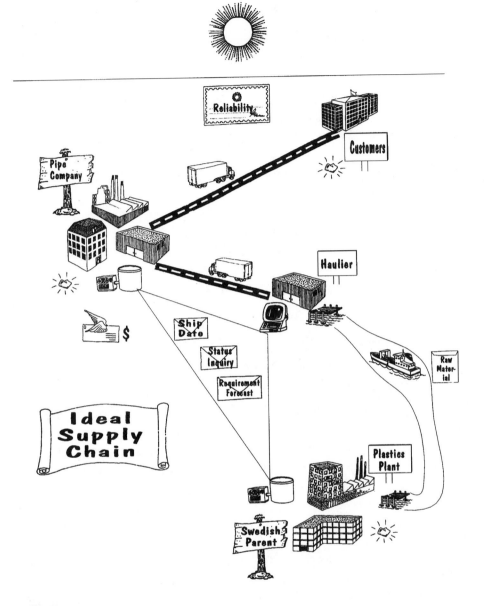

Labels in figure: Reliability, Customers, Pipe Company, Haulier, Ship Date, Status Inquiry, Requirement Forecast, Raw Material, Ideal Supply Chain, Plastics Plant, Swedish Parent

Figure 2.3.

inventory levels. You could ship pipe when you see that we need it and we wouldn't have to send you orders at all."

The Swedish distribution manager responded, "You're asking *me* to manage your inventory? Would you really trust me to do that?" Two people from the pipe company responded at the same time, "Just guarantee us a safety stock and keep us informed!" It seemed like the earth had moved and everybody was on their feet.

As the team was changing the map, the logistics manager said, "What this means to me is that we will try to keep inventory in Sweden low and keep yours high, reducing your risk of running out if there's some uncontrollable delay. I like it. We send the material when we can get good shipping prices and send invoices to you every month." The pipe company accountant broke in. "To make things simple, why don't you just keep ownership of all the raw material inventory until it is turned into pipe. We know the price because it is set on an annual basis. Every month, we'll just send you a check for what we've used." As the map was being changed everyone was smiling and talking animatedly to each other. They couldn't sit down.

In only a few minutes the map was changed to represent this shared ideal. The work steps of the supply chain had been cut to a fraction and responsibility was put in the hands of those who could best exercise control. Three people made a quick analysis showing the following savings:

- 35 percent in total inventory
- 20 percent lower transportation cost
- Elimination of all order handling costs
- Reduced risk of running out of stock
- Lower administrative costs to all parties

The only new cost was a data transmission facility between the two plants and writing the associated computer programs.

The group was excited by its innovations and wanted to implement them as soon as possible. The members developed an action plan and presentations to inform and gain authorization to proceed from the heads of the three companies. The changes were implemented within three months and the estimated benefits were exceeded. Members of the quality partnership team went on to focus on other problem areas and became a strong force for innovation and operations improvement.

Starting from three distinctly different positions, the group had eliminated their differences, established common objectives, and developed a plan in only two days. Rather than spending their time justifying their positions, the group members challenged and changed themselves. They eliminated the confrontational atmosphere and replaced it with joint purpose. Together they created a better solution than they ever could have imagined alone and implemented it very quickly. They solved their problem, renewed their spirits, and learned skills to apply elsewhere.

The train had crossed over the ravine. The bridge and its support timbers were now stronger than ever.

COMPARING THE TWO EXAMPLES

The results of Janice's supply chain project are so dramatically different from Matt's maintenance computer system project that we need to explore the reasons why. The challenges were similar: Both problems were complex and required creativity, but neither Matt nor Janice had enough knowledge of the entire problem to personally set a strategy. In both examples, the people with the information needed to solve the problem had diverse backgrounds and a history of difficulties in communication that were further complicated by a stress-filled atmosphere.

Matt met with the project team across a conference table. He couldn't overcome the communication barriers and differences of view, so he tried instead to solve the problem with a different group of people with whom he was more comfortable. The group members' lack of insights into the problem allowed their focus to wander and they eventually put their energy into damage containment rather than into the essence of the problem itself. When the decision was finally made, implementation was slow and costly because the project team felt no ownership for it.

Janice, on the other hand, met with her project team armed with a visual language tool. It helped her overcome the communication barriers and established an environment for creative thinking that led to remarkable results. The negative emotions surrounding the problem were transformed into positive energy and group vitality. Because the decision was jointly made, implementation was highly efficient.

Janice's example and Bill's example in chapter 1 show what visual languages can do. Section II will peel back the cover and try to show why they work.

SECTION II

WHY VISUAL LANGUAGES WORK

WHAT HOLDS
US BACK

T his chapter is the first of three that address the question of why visual languages work. It describes some of the small problems we encounter every day that can lead to much bigger problems. It gives each problem a name and a face to make it more memorable and easier to confront. There are two main sections. The first, "Personal Prisons," deals with problems inherent in our individual human nature and the second, "Organization Overcast," describes problems inherent in the structures we create.

PERSONAL PRISONS

We are subject to forces beyond our control that both define and confine us. Barriers of personality and experience separate and prevent us from communicating perfectly. Our personalities can be defined by four sets of preferences.[1]

1. How we interact with the world

2. How we gather data

3. How we make decisions

4. Life orientation

Preferences in each of the four areas define us into one of 16 personality types. Although there are a great many variations, the patterns are frequently a helpful guide to predicting behavior. Personal uniqueness may be an important asset, but it also acts as a prison. Prisons lock us in, but they also keep out people with personalities we don't like, reducing our ability to work in teams.

Our experiences are important parts of our prisons. The foundation was started by our parents, the roof was built by our teachers, and the walls were built by our peers and communities, but we built the bars ourselves. The first bar, for example, might have come from touching a hot stove. In one way or another, we add more bars daily. We can speak through the window to other people who are inside their own prisons, but we never connect completely.

Our prisons are not visible, sometimes not even to ourselves. It takes time for others to understand how yours is made. When we forget that we are prisoners and make assumptions that others see the world as we do, communications fail. We can rearrange the decor in prison, and in some instances may be transferred from one prison to another, but we can't break out.

Prison 1: Words Lost Between the Chairs

When we listen, we process one word at a time and translate the word into a thought using inner speech, a silent function that generates associations between the speaker's words and our concepts.[2] For efficiency, inner speech uses an abbreviated syntax and very few words, but it permits a variety of inner symbols to be associated with a given word. The symbol with which we connect the word is determined by what we have understood to be its context and this understanding may be faulty. The word *motherhood,* for example, might be used positively to refer to a period of a woman's life where she was very focused on giving aid and protection to her growing children, or it may be used negatively as an example of an unassailable quality that is not relevant to the task at hand.

Inner speech is completely egocentric, serving the self rather than others. When we speak, we draw on concepts that are formed by inner speech. When we are self-absorbed and not actively considering the context and needs of the listener, we may put our highly personalized vocabulary directly into words, omitting the context.

An example of this occurred when a secretary made a transatlantic plane reservation for his boss. He called the travel agency looking for the best fare price available between Zurich, Switzerland, and Tampa, Florida, and was told that special low-priced tickets were available. He said that his boss's schedule might need to change and asked, "Is there any restriction on changing?" The answer was "No."

When the boss arrived in Tampa she did indeed need to change her plans. She needed to go to New York before returning to Zurich. She went to a ticket agent to make the change and was told it was not possible because of the special ticket price. She would need to purchase an entire new ticket. "But I was assured that I could change my ticket if I needed to, with no charge!" The response was, "That's right, there is no charge for a *change* to a different flight from Tampa to Zurich, but you are asking for *rerouting,* and that is not allowed on this special ticket."

As with this example of the travel agent, we each have our special vocabulary, developed for good reasons. Sometimes a word has special meaning within a culture and it becomes so familiar that the prisoners forget that the meaning may not be shared by others.

Prison 2: Smug in Your Success

If you've worked hard, long, and well, people probably recognize your accomplishments.

You know how the world works and you know how to get along in the company. Your success is proof of that. You know the limits in your business and you don't get caught up in pursuing dreams that can't be brought to fruition. Your experience is valuable and justifies your position of responsibility. Other people come to you to ask whether their ideas are practical.

You may be a very pleasant and well-intentioned person, but at best you have developed a confidence that reduces your curiosity about the world and at worst an arrogance that insulates you from it. In other words, you are smug in your success.

In either case, without realizing it, you are much happier to confirm your myths and ideas than you are to challenge them. Your vanity and self-satisfaction encourage you to filter out inconvenient facts because they don't fit with the orderly, predictable world you see around you. You might ignore such facts, decide to think about them later, or react by challenging them with facts from your personal experience. Such filtering makes it more likely that you will build your new ideas on past realities. When you assume the old limits are still valid, and hear no facts that challenge them, your success may be failing you.

Prison 3: The Tyranny of Numbers

"The unquantified always suffers at the hands of the quantified." This old axiom is still with us today and may be a stronger influence than ever. Numbers are a precise and convenient means of measurement and description. When the subjective is made objective, it is easier to deal with and, as we saw in Bill's sales example in chapter 1, numbers and measures can be extremely useful in improving quality.

But, numbers are distracting, particularly when they are used to measure our performance. Numbers are definitive, uncompromising, and final and, if they will be used as measures, we treat them with respect and focus more on them than on subjective measures. In chapter 2, Matt fell victim to this and worried more about his numbers than about the people and processes needed to achieve them. We need numeric measures, but we need to keep them in perspective.

Prison 4: Tunneling

People want to achieve success and are willing to work hard. They keep their heads down and fight off distractions. As with any virtue, if carried to an extreme it causes problems. The intense concentration of tunneling devalues considerations in the big picture and the importance of aligning with the efforts of others.

Focusing intensely on objectives avoids time-wasting activities. Meeting with others and taking the time to hear and understand their views is a diversion to tunnelers, especially if they know that the others always come at problems from different directions.

In chapter 2, Matt didn't want to make the effort to bring his technical staff into his strategic discussions because they didn't speak his language, he didn't want to take the time to learn theirs and, most important, he didn't think they were coming at the problem from the right direction.

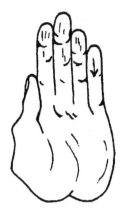

Prison 5: Not-Invented-Here

The not-invented-here (NIH) syndrome could be subtitled "If it's not my idea, I don't have time for it." NIH is so ingrained in some people and groups that it seems at times to be a reflex.

NIH sounds something like this: "Yes, I like your idea. It's really interesting. I agree we should do that sometime, but I'm quite busy for the next few months and couldn't get involved without. . . ." Whatever the specific wording, the meaning is, "Your idea is not a priority to me. I probably won't block you actively, but if my passivity blocks you, that's too bad." The underlying reason is a lack of ownership: "If it's your idea, it can't be mine. If it's not mine, I won't feel good about making it a reality." NIH is an emotional reaction and, with some people, logical arguments about the merits of ideas just don't work.

NIH impedes accomplishments, but is has other effects too. Sometimes people take the NIH reaction personally ("he thinks my ideas are no good, but won't say so"), and they become resentful. Other times, people criticize the NIH blocker for lacking empathy or imagination, having personal political considerations, or resisting change. These emotional reactions start a cycle of attitudes and behaviors that further destroy teamwork.

In order to avoid scaling down or abandoning their ideas, people often engage aggressively in company politics or seek ways to punish their blockers. Playing such games diverts energy from the task of satisfying customers. Initiative, risk taking, and productivity decline. NIH can grow from a small, all-too-human reflex to be an enormous obstacle to organizational effectiveness.

Prison 6: Why Change?

Change is fundamental to every business improvement. Change requires a decision to do something differently. Why do we change? Is it because we listen to the facts and understand the need and benefits of a different course of action? Sometimes, perhaps on little things, but not often on things that are important to us.

For example, a woman had smoked cigarettes since she was 16. As she prepared for marriage at age 21, her betrothed asked her to stop smoking when they were married. She agreed, but resumed her habit a short time after the wedding. For seven years she was subject to frightening facts, statistics, and her husband's reasons to stop. When she became pregnant, his arguments intensified and her doctor and friends added their own. Then, three months after the baby was born, without any immediate provocation, she decided to stop and never resumed the habit. Why? "Because one moment while I was holding my baby, I realized that I wanted to be with him as he grew up and became an adult and that, if I didn't stop smoking now, I might lose out."

In business situations, the personal nature of change is seldom as stark as this example. However, observations that most real change in companies takes place during or following a crisis is further evidence that change is emotional rather than intellectual. Unfortunately, organizations are ill-equipped to access and make use of their emotional resources. Our scientific and quantitative approach to achieving results has led to a culture that doesn't value emotion in the workplace and has not looked for tools to make use of it.

It is difficult to work together with others when we are locked in our prisons, communicating through barred windows with only our intellectual resources. If we could apply our emotional resources, perhaps we could bend the bars and get out into the prison yard.

ORGANIZATION OVERCAST

A second important class of human problems limiting enterprises' effectiveness has to do with how they align and motivate their members. Animals, and presumably our human ancestors, developed over the millennia a number of rituals of dominance and submission to maintain social order. This allowed tribes to focus on external threats and avoid wasting their energy on internal conflicts. Modern civilizations have struggled to find acceptable replacements for those humiliating rituals as their organizations have grown more complex. In businesses, carefully written position charters with definitions of financial and decision-making authority have evolved. In the 1990s business world, where levels of hierarchy are being removed and networks of peers are being called upon to run major parts of businesses, the old roles built on dominance and submission are no longer valid, but new ones are sometimes poorly defined and understood.

The term *organization overcast* refers to uncertainty about a member's role and authority. This vagueness saps motivation, energy, and drive from the member and from the whole. These everyday problems in life and at the office take their toll, holding us back from committing vigorously to a common purpose.

Cloud 1: The View Depends on Where You Sit

The cartoon above illustrates the importance of understanding or negotiating roles and responsibilities. Five birds are sitting on two wires while a sixth struggles to hold the ends together. The five are interested but are taking no action.

If the sixth bird were a manager, she might be feeling that she is the only one in the organization really working to make ends meet, that the others are just hangers-on who are not pitching in to help when they know they are needed. She is not in a position to take time to coach them on how to help her, and she may wish she could just let the wires drop and fly away from the situation.

The other five birds are not actively causing a problem and it may be that they don't know what to do to help. Perhaps they don't think helping is their job. Perhaps they think the manager reserved the critical task of holding the wires together as her own special duty, a way many managers treat strategic issues.

Whatever the reason, if the manager bird believes she has empowered her people, the message has apparently not been received and the organization is not running at anything near an optimum level.

Cloud 2: Soldiers in the New Army

This cartoon shows an army officer directing a soldier to get ready and to fire his weapon. After the shot is fired, the officer is out of the picture and the soldier looks perplexed.

As organization structures have flattened, managers have had to address a wider number of areas. They dart from one task to another, putting activities in motion and leaving other people to refine the direction and achieve results. The foot soldier in this cartoon is clearly not ready to carry out his mission.

Both the manager and the subordinate are using the same tools today as they have used for years. It may be that the officer set an abstract goal and the soldier doesn't understand enough of the big picture to decide what operational work should get priority. If he acts without full understanding of the task, he may need to undo or redo the work later. Other people may hold some of the knowledge he needs and he may not feel he has the authority needed to mobilize others. He may feel abandoned by his manager and resent him for putting him in a position where he is not effective.

Reducing management superstructure has led to many worthy results, such as putting authority closer to the task, but it has left some subordinates less effective than before because they don't have tools for communication and direction setting that work in the absence of line authority.

Cloud 3: The First Five Minutes

Many undertakings are doomed to fail from their inception. When looking back at an unsuccessful project, it is often clear that the failure could have been avoided by more effective communication in the first five minutes, when the manager and a subordinate should have reached a common understanding of the objectives of the endeavor, its scope, and the subordinate's role and expected behavior.

Role and behavior may be implied but not directly communicated or the meaning may get lost in the interpretation of words. When a manager assigns a project, the main topics of discussion are the task and its challenges. She may implicitly expect the subordinate to understand the style of behavior that the situation requires and adapt his most natural style accordingly. The subordinate may implicitly assume that if he has been given the assignment, it is not only because he has the right experience and other qualifications for it but also because his natural style is at least acceptable if not ideal. When a crisis comes, the conversation may go like this: "You knew this job was delicate and required a soft touch. You made a mess of it by going in there and pushing everybody around." (Meaning: "You're not very smooth and should be reduced in rank!")

"You're not being fair. When we started this project, you emphasized how quickly it had to be done and how much was at stake. You know how I operate. If you were so worried about somebody's nose getting out of joint, you should have said so." (Meaning: "You're changing the rules on me because you want the results but you don't want to take the heat. I won't trust you again.")

This kind of avoidable misunderstanding wastes organization energy and kills both morale and careers.

Cloud 4: The Fret Factor

When individuals are faced with complex issues, they hesitate before acting. Gathering the pertinent facts and reflecting is prudent, but prolonged delays, or fretting, can be expensive. Fretting is a triumph of thought and second thought over action, to one's own detriment.

One source of fretting is the complexity of analyzing all the possibilities. Thanks to computer services, we have an abundance of information available to us and the decision-making process can go like this.

- "What do the data tell us?"
- Review the data again.
- Ask for more data.
- Invite in experts.
- Let the data sit for a while.
- Review the data again.

Sometimes there are too little data and sometimes there seems to be conflicting data.

- "What should we do?"
- "Do we have to do anything?"
- "What would happen if we don't do anything?"

When the data don't point the way, our familiar decision-making processes and tools don't work and a mild form of panic sets in. Many people have not learned or have forgotten how to make decisions without data. Gut feelings or intuition are seldom applied in this information age, so decisions wait. We will torture the data until they confess.

A second source of fretting delays is when a manager can't see what her own new role would be after a contemplated change. "What will happen to me?" and "How will I fit in?" are the driving questions, even if they are not articulated. If you can't see yourself in a picture of the future, you can't move toward it. Many people are able to visualize in the negative sense (they worry) but they aren't able to create positive future images. They have no tools to help deal with such concerns on the human side of the issue.

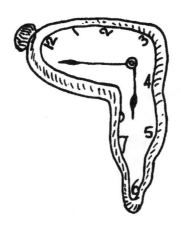

Cloud 5: Slip-Sliding

Sometimes objectives and direction are clearly set but, because of delays getting to action, they are modified or abandoned altogether. Even the most worthy objectives lose their ability to motivate over time. Either the opportunity slips away or the organization gets used to living with the problem and lets its priority slide.

You read in chapter 2 about how Matt's project objectives were greatly downscaled after long delays, and you have probably experienced slip-sliding yourself in other ways. Delays can be due to unavoidable external reasons and are sometimes a weapon employed by those who disagree to kill initiatives, but most often they are inadvertent and self-generated.

Slip-sliding has its roots in a lack of emotional commitment. Objectives that are abstract, imposed, or based on other people's ideas are subject to delays and abandonment. Delays occur because, in the absence of emotional drive, people invest their energy or risk their political capital only on the basis of personal cost/benefit. They may take the required actions but with little vigor. In the absence of emotional commitment, they easily rationalize away target dates when sacrifices are demanded. As delays accumulate, interest wanes.

An objective needs to be part of a compelling overall vision for people to invest their ingenuity and resources to overcome the inevitable obstacles. Without emotional commitment, time slips away unnoticed, opportunities and competitive position slip with it, and we wonder why.

> For all sad words of tongue or pen, the saddest are these:
> "it might have been!"[3]

SUMMARY

We tend to accept the elements of organization overcast as simply part of life at the office. When we recognize the elements at all, we think of them as small hindrances. We overlook them, but they quietly take their toll every day. Instead of finding ways to combat overcast, we put our attention on the secondary problems it creates.

A metaproblem underlying both personal prisons and organization overcast is the difficulty of employing emotional resources alongside intellectual resources. Effective communication, creative thinking, and teamwork require them both. Until we develop and apply generally accepted, systematic tools for this purpose, each of us will remain a less-than-ideal work partner and our organizations will not be able to fully summon and align the commitment of their members.

MOVING FROM IMAGES TO IMAGINATION

The evolution of culture is taking place at a rate that far exceeds the possibility of biological adaptation and can severely test our evolved capacities.[1] A number of medical researchers now work alongside evolutionary biologists and are developing a new field of study called *Darwinian medicine.*[2] Looking backward in time, they are finding that the diagnosis of some diseases is aided by better understanding of the evolution of the human body. For example, human physiological responses to recent changes in food sources and eating habits have been found to explain some causes of coronary diseases and cancers. If evolution gives clues to some modern physical ailments, perhaps it might give useful clues to some ailments of modern organizations.

This chapter includes a selection of research findings that try to explain aspects of the way we think, communicate, and work together today in order to help understand a few of the limitations to organization effectiveness and how to overcome them. It focuses on our sense of sight, particularly on why it is able to help access our emotional resources, creativity, and capacity for teamwork.

Readers who are primarily interested in the applied, practical aspects of applying visual language may choose to skip this chapter.

PHYSICAL REACTIONS TO COLOR

Human beings have distinctive, measurable reactions to the sight of different colors, and their preferences for different colors are excellent predictors of elements of their personalities. A few examples provide a glimpse of how genetic heritage affects our behavior.

When people are exposed to red, their nervous systems are measurably stimulated. Blood pressure rises, respiration and heartbeat speed up. Similar exposure to dark blue has the reverse effect: blood pressure falls, heartbeat and breathing slow down. Why should red stimulate and dark blue calm us? Max Lüscher asserts that the origins of these reactions and the inborn significance that some colors hold for us go back millions of years in our evolution to the early humans' reactions to day, night, and other features of life.[3]

Red, the color of blood, is the dominant color of the hunt and calls all resources to high alert. The dark blue of the night sky is the color of quiet and passivity and there is a general slowing of metabolic activity that precedes sleep. Yellow, the color of the sun, is the color of hope and activity. Measured physical reactions to these colors are remarkably similar in all people, including those who are color blind.

Advertising specialists are keenly aware of color's powerful effects on our moods and attitudes and exploit them to communicate to our emotions in order to attract us to their products. Color also could play a useful role in finding the means of accessing and applying the emotional resources of an organization.

BRAIN HEMISPHERE SPECIALIZATION AND PREFERENCE

Recent scientific research has uncovered a great deal about how the brain functions and has led to physical explanations of some human capabilities and behavior. The left- and right-brain hemispheres have different specialties.[4]

Left	*Right*
• Words	• Images
• Sequential processing	• Simultaneous processing
• Analysis	• Synthesis
• Logic	• Intuition

In the same way that a person is left- or right-handed, there appears to be a preference for working from either the left- or right-brain hemisphere. This is not surprising as we also have preferences for a single foot, eye, and ear. This orientation affects each person's approach to the world, priorities, style of gathering information, thinking, solving problems, and communicating.

Tests show that natural preferences are in total about evenly divided between the left and right sides.[5] However, Western society and organizations value the left-brain skills more than the right. Science, mathematics, facts, analysis, and their associated values are more prized in organizations than, for example, intuition, emotion, and imagination. There are historical reasons for left-brain dominance of organization life, mainly that science and engineering have been the main forces behind the rise of the economically advanced societies. There may also be behavioral reasons: Those people who most aspire to structure and control their environment tend to be left-brain dominant. In addition, there may be physiological reasons. Because language is such a critical, basic part of human functioning, it is nearly always active, dominating thinking activities so that other left-brain orientations are more easily ascendant.

Whatever the reason, the dichotomy between the even split between left and right preferred thinking styles and the strong dominance of the left in business operations suggests that there is an opportunity to enhance organizational performance through more effective employment of the relatively underutilized right brain. Competitive factors are starting to increase the value put on creativity, but intuition, which could also add to the effectiveness of process redesign and other business challenges, remains undervalued.[6]

EVOLUTION OF THE BRAIN

The Triune brain theory holds that the human brain developed in three main stages.[7] There is a hierarchy, where the older parts dominate the whole when safety and other basic needs are not being met.

The oldest part, the stem or reptilian brain, is at the top of the spinal column and is the core of the brain. It is believed to contain some ancient instincts and perform basic functions such as maintaining wakefulness and filtering information coming from the senses. First impressions, for example, are part of a memory system that takes information from the eyes, seeks recognition, and generates emotional reactions before the newer parts of the brain know about the input. These impressions are independent from reason and are not overlaid by later experience.[8] This may explain why our first impressions are lasting, even if contradicted by later experience or logical analysis.

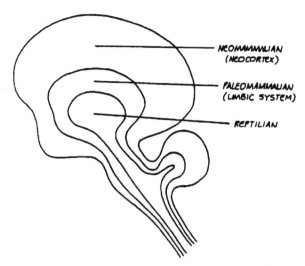

Reprinted with permission from Ned Hermann, author of *The Creative Brain,* page 30.

When a visual image is recognized as danger, the brain stem takes control. It increases heartbeat and muscle tension and triggers a rush of adrenaline to the blood stream which causes a set of sensations we call *fear,* including that feeling of emptiness in the pit of your stomach. Lower mammals respond with a fight/flight response where the brain stem responds from a preexisting, genetically programmed set of behaviors.[9] It is not unlikely that other more subtle behavior patterns are triggered in humans when their eyes perceive images that are somehow threatening.

The limbic system developed next and encircles the primitive brain. It plays critical roles in emotion and motivation. Together with the primitive brain, it is similar to the brains of lower animals and is thought to control instinctive behaviors such as migration, follow-the-leader rituals, hierarchies of dominance-submission, defending territory, ganging up on the new or weak, bonding, and flocking.[10] It appears that emotional states centered in the limbic system can dominate higher-order reasoning, similar to the way the primitive brain is able to seize control of total brain functioning under danger circumstances. People in love, for example, are noted for perceiving and acting in ways that seem not to be logical.

The modern brain, or neocortex, overlays the limbic system. It is adept at learning new ways of coping and adapting and is the seat of higher-order thinking.

The brain's evolution suggests that the limbic system and its role in emotions may play a critical, if not generally recognized, role in organization effectiveness. Any methods that can help us access and actively employ parts of the older brain's functionality would be of great value in improving our ability to work better together.

EVOLUTION OF THE VISUAL SENSE AND ITS IMPACT ON THINKING

Mankind developed keen eyesight probably because of the thousands of generations our distant ancestors spent as tree dwellers.[11] In a forest canopy, identifying good branches to jump from and to meant survival, so evolution favored visual acuity and depth perception. Later, when the climate changed and the forest thinned, our (presumed) ancestors moved to the ground. They started walking on two legs in part because it gave them the advantage of being able to see much greater distances than their four-legged competitors, who generally depended on their sense of smell. As a result, humans were better able to avoid dangers and take advantage of opportunities.

Humans apparently at one time had the capability of eidetic imagery, the ability to maintain a strong, full-color, visual image of a scene and recall it in detail for days afterward. Many children today are capable of eidetic imagery, but most of them in the West lose this capacity as they mature, perhaps because our educational systems are based on words and the ability of eidetic imagery is not used.[12] Some adults, however, are able to draw on eidetic memory in situations when they are intensely and emotionally interested and can describe scenes in great detail, even many years later. While this capability can be useful, like memory in general, it has become less valued as books, photographs, and other media have become available.

Eidetic imagery retains a place in some African tribes. Some witch doctors have the ability to form a three-dimensional image in front of them that is so real that they can touch it and describe it so vividly that others, adults and children alike, can see it and react emotionally to it.[13]

Carl G. Jung and other psychologists have alerted us to the existence of symbols in human dreams that are common to cultures around the world and seem to be wired into our subconscious minds.[14] We can speculate that those symbols evolved from the brain's use of eidetic images to respond to dangers and other challenges of life at an early stage of human development.

Building from the capacity to recall images, the ability to manipulate them may have developed and led to the building of abstract images and then to the creation of symbols. Searching for symbols in images may be the origin of human thinking capacity and the source of our creativity.

THE BRAIN'S VISUAL MAPS

When a frog sees an insect flying, it immediately recognizes it as food and reacts at lightning speed. The same frog, however, will die of starvation even if it is surrounded by dead insects. The dead insects could keep it alive, but the frog doesn't recognize them as food. Scientists asked why during the 1960s but didn't have answers. Later research showed that the frog's and other animals' brains come equipped at birth with maps of some things that are vital to survival, such as food or predators.[15] Apparently, there is no map for a stationary insect, so it can't be identified as food.

In lower forms of life, all maps are wired in genetically. In higher animals, maps apparently can be updated or built over a lifetime so that, for example, from a visual pattern match with only a portion of an image such as the back of a head, a full map of the face and its associated body can be immediately summoned to generate recognition.

Some aspects of intuition apparently function in a similar manner. From a facial expression or small action, an entire visual or emotional map can be summoned that projects a total context and expected consequence. This would explain how intuitive people can be both rapid and highly accurate in judgments without being able to explain the logic behind their insights. This view argues for a more appropriate and synergistic balance of intuition and reason in organization life.

MIND–BODY UNITY

A recent study of the effect of the mind on physical health yielded some new ways of understanding the relationship between the mind and body that have implications for the effectiveness of people in organizational settings. Some points made by noted medical doctors and psychiatrists include[16]

- Emotion appears to have an effect on the immune system. For example, deaths peak the days after Christmas and after the Chinese new year. Very happy and very sad states both enhance the immune system. People who feel isolated have three to five times the mortality rate of others.

- Emotion plays an important role in healing. Laughter, humor, and feeling good are part of healing. Fear and anger reduce the ability to control and tolerate pain and appear to negate the effects of medications. Physical touching can be seen to increase the will to live, in babies and in adults.

- Body and mind have not been considered as a single entity in Western cultures since the 16th century, at the start of the scientific era. René Descartes, who wished to avoid being excommunicated from the church, as his contemporary Galileo had been, made an agreement with the Vatican that he would study science and that the church would be responsible for the soul. This separation of mind from body remains to this day and is responsible for the absence of a common vocabulary between psychology and medicine.

- There is intelligence throughout the body. It is not uniquely concentrated in the brain. There are neuropeptides, the biochemicals of the brain and emotions, in every cell in the body. They act like satellite receivers for messages from the brain. They direct where the body should put its energy. They affect blushing and other physical changes. Emotions and feelings, not the intellect and reason, are the links between the mind and body. Many emotions are stored in the body and don't percolate to the brain.

Thinking was a great advantage for early humans, but it did not take place in offices or conference rooms. It was combined with actions. Interworking of people was also part of this action-thinking in hunting, defense, or shelter building. This argues that both thinking and interworking would be facilitated by physical activity.[17]

Business organizations envy the interworking skills of sports teams but are quick to say that comparing the two is like apples and oranges: Sports teams have clear goals and tasks, they can practice their repertoire of plays regularly, they receive immediate feedback on mistakes, they know who the opposition is, what the rules are, and when they are succeeding. But, when human evolution is considered, closer examination shows a few simple but important lessons businesses could learn from sports: The team is more powerful than the sum of the members because its shared history of intense emotional experiences forms bonds of trust and caring. Sports teams actively combine the intellectual tasks of strategy with the physical, spatial tasks of shooting, passing, throwing, or hitting. Emotion is not only accepted but encouraged. (Everyone knows that winners are psyched and that an underdog can pull out the big one on guts alone!)

The "talking heads" controversy that arose during the 1992 U.S. presidential campaign gives insights into the importance of physical and emotional factors in communication. Although distaste for talking heads had surfaced earlier in the public consciousness, it reached the level of national discussion during the campaign. As was widely reported, the public was profoundly dissatisfied listening to the disembodied head of a television news analyst explaining events and candidates' positions in intellectual terms. Presumably the public needed other information to fully understand what the candidates stood for. Ratings showed that audiences preferred getting information directly from the candidates, seeing them full length including their gestures, expressions, and tones of voice.

Suppressing emotion and limiting physical activity may be as bad for organization health as it would be for personal health. Communicating words and numbers gets the facts out but leaves our gut instincts locked away. Not acknowledging them may lead to elaborate logical justification that is not rooted in understanding of the emotions behind them. Talking at each others' suits across the table may be good for decorum but doesn't help teamwork. Stiff settings lead to building masks rather than real commitment.

Communication and teamwork are strongly affected by the visual sense, emotion, and physical movement. A language of visual symbols joined with a physically active group process can draw power from all three.

VISUAL THINKING

Rudolph Arnheim, an authority on artistic expression, asserts that thinking and perceiving are very closely linked.[18] He points out that the basic elements of thinking, including exploring, focusing, grasping of essentials, comparing, separating, combining, putting in context, and problem solving occur not only when a person sits with eyes closed and thinks, but also when he simply looks directly at the world. He explains that thoughts need shape and words are valuable only because they can summon visual imagery.

When dealing with complex tasks, your thinking is in highly abstract images that may occur below the level of consciousness. If you are conscious of them, they may be hard to describe and easily disturbed. As ideas start to form, specific images are taken from memory to fill out the abstract image. If you were creating a marketing plan, for example, you would summon images of target customers, ideal products, and promotion methods and form a composite image. Creative flashes occur when specific images are selected that fill in and complete the abstract model or establish a new model.

The most complex problems are often solved by creating a visual metaphor that relates the problem solution to some commonly understood phenomenon. The most famous example of this is Albert Einstein's discovery of the theory of relativity by imagining himself traveling on a light beam and observing certain phenomena.

If you are fortunate and have an extraordinary mind like Einstein, you can pack your memory with information and, after a germination period, a metaphor will show itself that organizes the information into a powerful new idea. Regardless of the quality of your mind, this process can be very long and tends to work best in solitude.

When people of normal capabilities need to involve others and need speed, they are best served by packing their communal visual memory with all available facts in the form of images or pieces of images and using a metaphor readily available to organize the information into new ideas that they will jointly own.

THE FIRST VISUAL LANGUAGE

When humans first sought a communication method other than speaking, they developed a visual language. Egyptian hieroglyphics is one of the oldest known written languages. It was first used more than 5000 years ago and remained in active use for more than 4000 years. In ancient Egypt there was a strong interrelationship between art and writing. The hieroglyphs themselves are miniature pictures and their use led to an extremely rich language.

Two aspects of this language are particularly interesting. First, each hieroglyph followed the rules of Egyptian art and very strong symbolism was employed. Egyptian art was not free form, it had strict rules of presentation and was intended to make those things depicted live forever. Egyptians believed that divine words could be created using hieroglyphs that could give or take away power from humans, birds, or animals.[19] Each thing or portion of it was portrayed with great fidelity in its most characteristic aspect. As a result, in a picture of a man's body, although the arms, legs, and torso are each accurately represented and immediately recognizable, the picture of a whole man looks distorted and unnatural to us. This approach was drawn upon in the early 20th century by Pablo Picasso and Georges Braque in their cubist style of painting which fragmented the subject into cubes and viewed each from an independent perspective, thus providing three-dimensional information on their canvases.

Second, some classes of hieroglyph had both a symbolic and a phonetic value. For example, an image of a man in a certain pose represents *master* and the sounds *nb*. A bird means *in* and was pronounced *m,* while an abstract enclosure represented a *house* and was pronounced *pr.*

nb   *m*   *pr*

The Master is in the house.

These usages made the language open to nuance and the medium challenged people to think more actively about their grammar than we do today when using Western languages. The Egyptians resisted transformation of their language to a simpler alphabetic form. Some attempts were made and abandoned, presumably because words written with letters lost the visually distinctive patterns that enhance hieroglyphics' legibility. In addition, the use of visual symbols gave the language a relatively large number of signs which would have been sacrificed to simplification. It may also have been seen as causing the language to lose its magical, life-affecting properties.

European languages relied exclusively on letters and words to represent sounds and record verbal speech. This was a versatile way of communicating complex thoughts. Words and numbers became the language of science and, when mechanical printing technologies were invented, the direction of Western written language was set.

DIRECTIONS FOR NEW VISUAL LANGUAGES

We possess a thought process based on meaning-laden images but use a communication process based on strings of meaning-free letters that requires intellectual decoding. Decoding is tacked onto our native method of thinking and can cause errors. While spoken words have limited ability to convey emotions, written words are still less efficient because they lose the accompanying messages passed through voice tones, facial expressions, and other body language.

Words are our allies and have been the foundation of civilization's progress, but this accumulation of evidence argues that we should supplement verbal with visual communication whenever we are faced with great complexity and the need for creativity. It also argues that we should recognize that our physical and emotional nature plays a role in thinking and communication effectiveness.

These findings suggest the need for more visual and physically active tools to help us work better together. Chapter 5 puts forth a set of principles to guide the development of such tools.

FOUNDATION PRINCIPLES FOR VISUAL LANGUAGE

Visual language is a means to pass messages using symbols, but it can be much more. It can be a tool to help people understand and come to agreement about complex issues, think clearly together about where they should go, and unite in common cause. As such, it can be an organization effectiveness tool and provide the base for functioning in flat, lean organizations.

This chapter defines 10 principles for building visual languages that draw from both research and practical experience.

1. Make your issue mind-sized.

2. Put clarity before purity.

3. Tell picture stories.

4. Employ both words and images.

5. Anchor your analysis.

6. Raise the bar to break constraints.

7. Put your child to work.

8. Open the dialogue to all stakeholders.

9. Build a map to build a team.

10. Steer by your maps.

Following these principles can help you send clearer messages through the bars of your personal prison, blow away some of the overcast, and help your organization renew itself.

Principle 1: Make Issues Mind-Sized

Problems that are not acted upon may eventually produce disasters. Opportunities left unexplored go to competitors. Sometimes we don't address problems and opportunities because they are vague, fuzzy, and amorphous.

Just as food needs to be bite-sized to be chewed and digested, problems must be mind-sized before they can be solved. A problem is mind-sized when it

1. Can be defined

2. Can be communicated clearly to others

3. Motivates them to action

A problem is not mind-sized if

1. Its dimensions or its implications are unclear

2. Its consequences are too small to be disturbing

3. It takes a backseat to other priorities

4. Those involved can't see themselves in the solution

Process problems that involve many people or groups are often very complex. They may stay undefined simply because people don't know how to go about clarifying them or because the effort required appears too great. Having a tool available for this purpose can be the catalyst needed to make the issue mind-sized and move the group to solve it.

Principle 2: Put Clarity Before Purity

You might argue that the label on the bottle on the left side contains more information, but you would have to agree that only the one on the right is mind-sized. It has defined the problem (poison), it has communicated it (instantly, with no intellectual processing needed), and it has motivated action (in this case negative action, don't touch).

Images reduce our dependence on words for communication. They are a direct means of communicating that don't require listening skills, language skills, or patience. They confront the viewer with a great deal of information at the same time. The viewer can choose where to focus, the sequence and length of concentration on different aspects of the message.

Images are an effective means of clarifying complex issues. When problem situations have multiple layers and nets of interdependencies, our traditional analytical methods and sequential reasoning are very slow to find solutions. Images engage the right brain's ability to synthesize many factors at the same time, allowing us to draw immediate conclusions. The following example is not complex, but shows the point.

If A is smaller than B, and
    B is greater than C, and
    B is smaller than D, and
    D is greater than E, and
    D is greater than F, then D is the largest.

However, when the facts are turned into an image, the communication is much faster and the logical analysis takes place at the moment you look at the image.

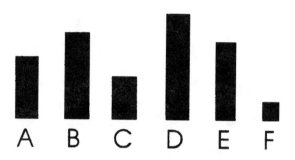

The importance of putting clarity before purity grows in importance as situations become more complex. An example of this is the map of the London Underground railroad system. This map may be the most successful in the world based on its impact on others of its kind. Although its format is very familiar now on subway and bus maps around the world, the map used to look different. It was precise about distances and directions and was very difficult to read, especially in the central area.

In 1931 a draftsman, Henry Beck, who had been laid off by the London Underground set himself the task of improving the map to fill his spare time.[1] Sitting at his kitchen table, he decided that the existing maps weren't adequate because they didn't put their priority on what people really want to know when it concerns public transit: What line should I take? Where should I get off? What is the stop just before I need to get off?

To simplify the map, Beck used the Thames River as the horizontal axis to give the map visual unity (see Figure 5.1). He identified the different transit lines by color and used only 90- and 45-degree angles for visual simplicity.

He was rehired by the London Underground later that year and the map was immediately published. The fact that distances between stops were not to scale, the directions were not exact, and the location of train stops were rough approximations troubled riders not at all and his concepts were borrowed by cities all over the world.

Henry Beck identified and focused on the essential needs of an underground train rider and the resulting clarity produced a map of much greater utility. He violated certain presumed rules of communication, but was better able to achieve his goal.

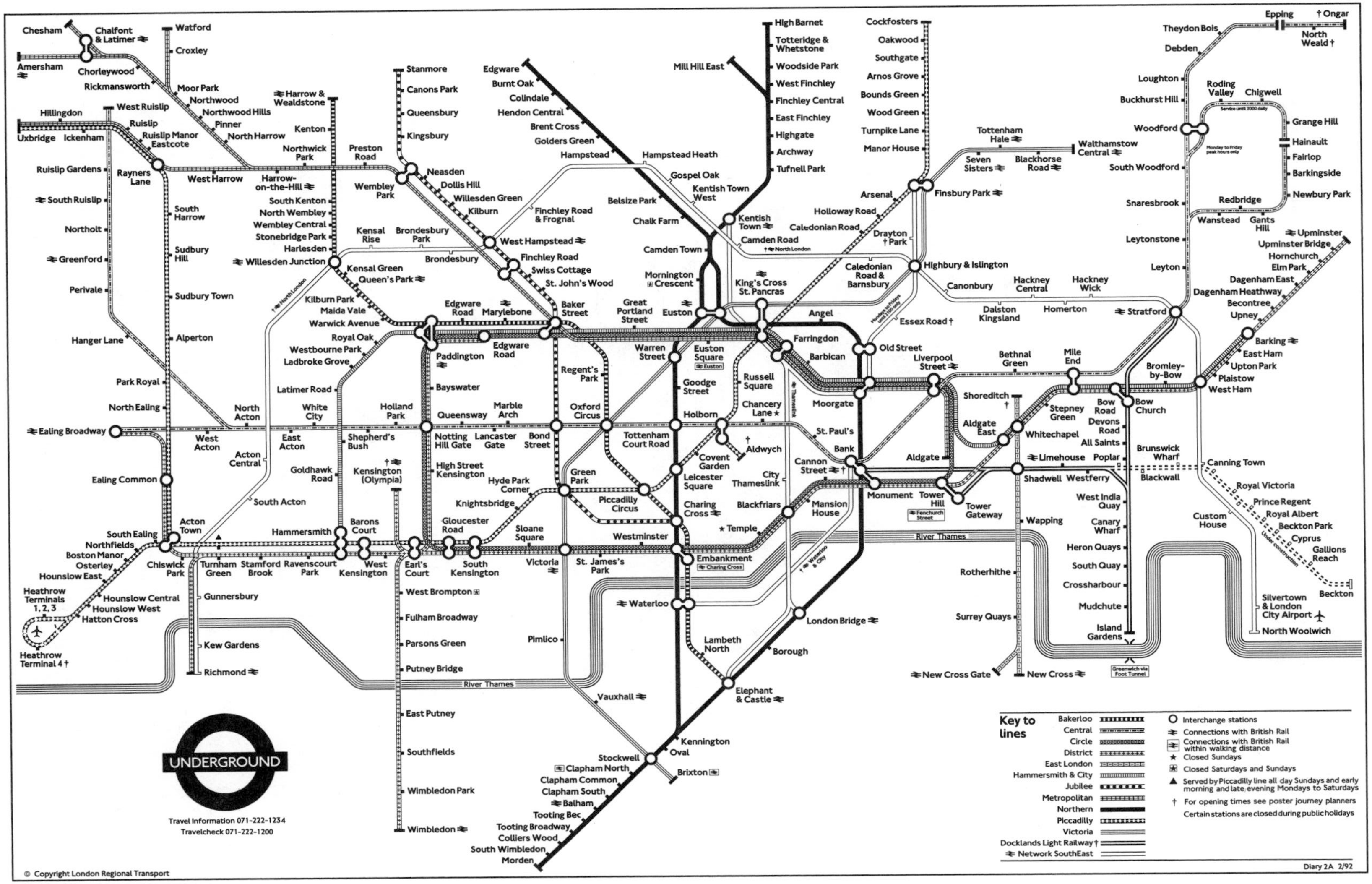

LRT Registered User No. 94/E/604.

Figure 5.1

73

Clearer expression permits clearer thinking, and clearer thinking permits clearer expression. When situations are driven by human relationships and emotions, words become less adequate and conventional logic may not function at all. Images can be most valuable in such a case because they address all of the behavioral problems noted in chapter 4 and open the door to applying the principles that follow.

Principle 3: Tell Picture Stories

This drawing is a copy of a page from the notebook of an alchemist in the Middle Ages. Like all good scientists, alchemists recorded their experiments but, in their case, they didn't want others to be able to use their experiments to leapfrog them in their quest to turn lead into gold. The problem was how to remember what they had done before but not let the information be accessible to others. The answer of many alchemists was to record the experiment as a picture story and then lock the notebook away in a vault. Because it was recorded in visual symbols, it could be recalled easily long after the fact.

The picture story shows a process for purifying gold. The dead king represents a gold alloy. The gray wolf, antimony sulfide, devours the dead king. When the wolf is burned on a pyre (or evaporated over a Bunsen burner), a live king, purified gold, returns.[2]

Three important lessons are present in this drawing. First, symbols can be used to tell a story, making a powerful and memorable visual image. Second, the picture story can show time and sequence. Third, a story can add a dimension of play to serious work.

A visual metaphor or picture story can provide a syntax for a symbol vocabulary. If well chosen, the metaphor will be vivid and memorable and provide a rich vocabulary.

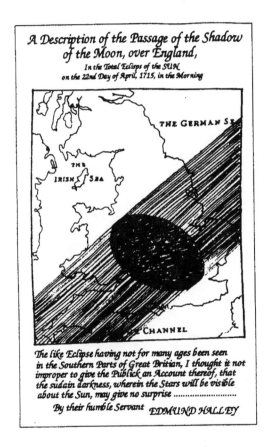

Principle 4: Employ Both Words and Images

Edmund Halley, the famous astronomer for whom the comet is named, had another reason to use visual aids. In 1715 he predicted a solar eclipse centered on the heart of the English realm. Fearing that it would be interpreted by the masses as an evil omen for King George, his patron, he wrote a treatise predicting the occurrence and explaining it as a natural phenomenon. Because the great majority of his countrymen couldn't read, he also drew a map to go with the treatise.[3]

This message, a portion of which is adapted here, proved to be highly effective. It shows how the combination of images and written explanation can be far superior to either by itself. It shows the big picture, relationships, time, and detail that could not be made visual at the same time. Its appeal may come in part from drawing on both right- and left-brain thinking styles.

Halley's message to those setting out to create effective visual language is: Words and images together make the clearest statement. Maps built with symbols are full of meaning for those who created them, but most of their richness is lost on an outside observer if they are not explained.

In addition, some groups will include people who do not quickly take to working with images and would prefer to work with written words. Because the visual language process should provide for recording the key visual messages in text form, these people can take on that task and be more comfortable.

Principle 5: Anchor Your Analysis

When confronted with a problem, people naturally want a solution. It is less natural to want to take the time to understand and gain consensus on the exact nature of the problem. Impatience and speed usually result in delaying a real solution because the wrong problem is addressed, arguments ensue, and only partial solutions can be agreed upon. When problems involve complex processes, it is nearly certain that no individual understands the whole. Each stakeholder understands her or his piece and has only a notional idea of the rest—or worse, has misinformation about it.

Procedures for using visual languages can be constructed to over-come the tendency to jump to solutions and ensure a higher-quality end result. The message of anchoring is twofold.

1. Structure the process to require complete understanding of the current state before addressing the future. If common agreement cannot be reached on the relatively concrete issues of where you are today and where there are difficulties, old conflicts will drift into new visions and any new agreement on how things should be in the future will likely quickly become unraveled.

   From a language mechanics point of view, it is also beneficial to start with the current state. The task of building a model of a known reality is a much easier task than giving explicit form to future visions without benefit of a reference point.

2. Before sailing off to a solution, use the language's process to saturate the group with facts and emotional messages about today's real-life situation. This stimulation, visually given and recorded, is the stuff from which creativity springs. Solutions that are not anchored will be lacking in innovation or incomplete and impractical. If you do not take the time to understand today's paradigms, you will not challenge them.

Principle 6: Raise the Bar to Break Constraints

When we make assumptions or are smug about our current approach, we are limiting the chances of finding a creative solution. The raise-the-bar principle requires that objectives be set so high that all assumptions have to be questioned in order to find a solution. Some people will argue that goals have to be reasonable and attainable to be motivating, but when was new ground broken without outrageous thinking or behavior? Innovation, by definition, goes outside traditional ways of looking at things.

Innovation is easier said than done. If "necessity is the mother of invention," how can we invent during a time of comfort? History is full of examples where extreme circumstances generated innovation and initiative that never would have arisen otherwise. Some civilizations developed and flourished largely because they faced serious problems.

To break out of constraints, you have to first see and recognize them for what they are. For many years, the greatest limiting factor on the height attained by pole-vaulters was not physical strength or technique but the unchallenged assumption that everyone needed to employ the same pole, a pole developed with the technology options available generations earlier. Defying tradition and using a revolutionary fiberglass pole allowed John Pennel to become the first person in the world to jump 17 feet in 1963, leaving competitors with standard poles in the dust.

One way to raise the bar is to set high targets. Another is to widen the scope of the problem being addressed. Still another is to demand a solution in a short time. In today's organizations, looking beyond your own department and seeing your customers as part of your processes not only leads to higher creativity but also to higher quality and customer satisfaction. Achieving results quickly gives competitive advantage.

Principle 7: Put Your Child to Work

We know that our personal prisons limit our creativity. Each of our experiences leaves us a bit of wisdom that can help us throughout our careers and some ideas that limit our thinking about what is possible and how to accomplish things. Because we can't be certain what will be tomorrow's wisdom and what will be its self-limiting thinking, we need to lock away all our experiences for a while if we want to enter a state of mind that is fertile for creativity. This may go against your adult grain, but you need to enter a childlike state where you ask dumb questions, challenge all limits, and try things that others know can't be done if you are to discover a new idea.

At the same time, you need to be purposeful and keep your attention squarely fixed on the issue at hand. Your child can approach the issue in a different way and may find an answer that has escaped you earlier. You will have plenty of opportunities to return to your adult state and test your fresh ideas against your accumulated experiences.

Visual language helps you release the child inside because metaphors and visual symbols are playlike. You may be rusty, but you do know how to play and, in play, you will find that you are open to suggestions from your friends, listen better, and are not too quick to criticize. People who think that play is a waste of time in the adult world probably achieve fewer results even though they talk more about them.

Principle 8: Open the Dialogue to All Stakeholders

Stakeholders are those people directly concerned with an issue or process. They have a stake, in that they participate in its functioning or are affected by its result. Their intimate knowledge of the issue and its components and the fact that they will have to live with the result make them better able and more committed to solve problems than their organizational superiors or outside experts.

Nevertheless, many times the stakeholders are not the ones to solve their own problems because management thinks they don't have the skills, perspective, or time needed. Sometimes, they are given the responsibility, but they fail because they are "soldiers in the new army" or, because of other organization behavior problems, they don't communicate well or they can't reach consensus. To be effective, stakeholder groups need tools.

Visual languages are tools that improve communication and stimulate a high level of creativity. With them, stakeholders can be the most efficient and effective problem solvers anywhere. The following example, taken from experiences in a research project sponsored by the University of the Philippines and the Ministry of Health, demonstrates this.[4]

Although it is a health matter of little consequence in the West, diarrhea continues to kill more than five million children each year in the rest of the world. It is a problem in the Philippines and in the early 1980s was a particular problem in a small fishing village on a remote island there. It was not the diarrhea itself that was the problem, it was that the diarrhea peaked there at a different time than everywhere else.

The regional health service arranged special logistics operations to deliver oral rehydration salts to remote villages during the rainy season, when occurrences of the disease were expected. In this village, however, diarrhea struck children most in the sunny season, months after the salts had been delivered. Because of the heat and humidity in the region, the salts had by then become rock hard and were useless.

Although this was a recurring problem, the causes were not understood, special deliveries of salts were prohibitively expensive, and the problem was long ignored. Finally, a medical team was sent to study the problem but could reach no conclusion. The following year, a specialist was dispatched but he could not find the cause either. The next year, a Ph.D. candidate visited the village as part of a research project to help villages monitor their health conditions. He invited the local midwives to meet with him to develop tools to organize and analyze their health and social-economic data.

The first tool they developed, shown in Figure 5.2, was a map of the village showing the houses where the cases of diarrhea had occurred during the past year. The second tool, shown in Figure 5.3, was a graph of occurrences by month. The fourth tool, shown in Figure 5.4, was an illustrated calendar mapping the year in terms of familiar activities and

Figure 5.2

rhythms of life. It showed the cycles of rany/sunny seasons, fishing/fish drying seasons, planting/harvesting, religious occasions, and fiesta.

With the three images now in front of the group, the student asked them what could be happening to cause diarrhea to peak during the sunny season and not the rainy season as it did everywhere else on the

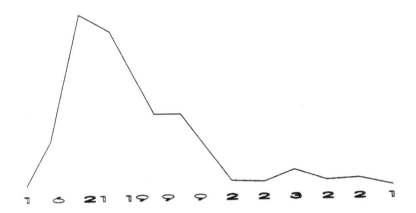

Figure 5.3

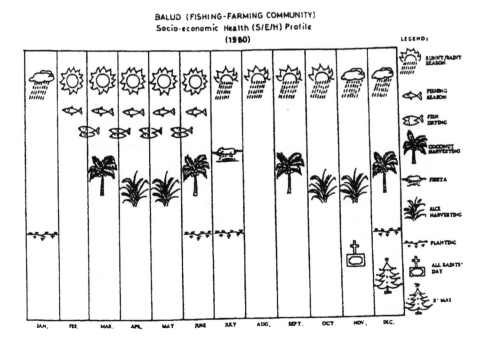

Figure 5.4

island. They looked intensely at the images, stood, pointed, walked around, and discussed it for five minutes. Then, in great excitement, first one and then all shouted the answer: "It's the fish drying!"

The villagers were overwhelmed by the discovery of their capability to understand and explain a matter of great importance with the humble and simple facts available to them. Using these skills, they would be able to save the lives of many children! Their tears and joy were so strong that discussion could not resume for a half hour.

They then explained to the student that the mothers in this village were conscious of their childrens' cleanliness and watched carefully what they ate. During the sunny season, however, the men were very busy fishing and fish drying and all the women of the village were required to work in the fields. They were away from home for three to five days at a time. "We leave the oldest child in charge, but during the day there are no adults around who watch the children. Eventually they disobey, play near the fish-drying area, which has many flies around, and eat pieces of fish from the racks." The source of the problem was in the environment and social system of the village, not in the disease itself.

Now that the problem was understood, the solution could be addressed. It did not come out of medical research, it came out of a group problem-solving process. The midwives met with the village leaders and explained the problem. Their visual tools helped the fishermen quickly understand and they agreed to move the fish-drying stands away from the village. The old women then volunteered to watch over the children during the day while the mothers were away working in the fields.

In this example, a problem that had eluded experts with advanced training and scientific equipment was clarified in just a few minutes by problem stakeholders who used visual tools. Their simply constructed maps of time and location helped give them a systemic view that linked the symptom of the problem, diarrhea, to who had it and where. The maps prompted them to ask the key questions of what was happening in those families' environment and in the community that could be contributing to the health problem. The tools helped make the problem mind-sized by showing its context, allowing them to synthesize a lot of data at one time, valuing their experience, and encouraging them to use their intuition. The tools permitted full involvement of people who had until then stayed on the sidelines. The knowledge they already possessed and the thinking skills they didn't realize they had were all it took to solve the problem of sunny season diarrhea.

Principle 9: Build a Map to Build a Team

When an issue has been defined and stakeholders have been empowered to solve it, the question arises of how to approach it. The stakeholder group may be small but, for issues that cross over many functions, it may include 20 or more people. Large groups often are very inefficient at solving broad issues.

The group members may remain together and try to talk out the problem or they may split themselves into separate groups that study some aspect of the problem in detail before reporting back. Either way, as time slides by and the problem remains unsolved, a new set of problems is created: the out-of-pocket expenses and the time they are away from the job trying to find the solution.

Visual languages allow large groups to work efficiently by having them build maps together. Building in small groups provides a high degree of participation, and presenting and discussing maps is an efficient means of looking at all sides of an issue and reaching consensus.

The function of building is esteemed by all societies and people find it personally satisfying to create a visible end product. When addressing organization problems, the work of building together can create a positive goal-oriented atmosphere, the pride of a shared creation, and ownership. Building requires dozens or hundreds of small physical acts of assistance. These patterns of mutual support carry over to everyday activities and lead to effective teamwork. A group that builds its solutions together leaves no place for NIH.

Principle 10: Steer by Your Maps

We often place pictures of our families on our desks to remind ourselves of our priorities in life. Many self-help books say that the way to achieve your life's ambitions is to draw a picture of how you will feel once you have become a millionaire or won a Nobel Peace Prize and put it in a place where you will see it often. Focusing your attention with visual images guides your actions toward a goal, even if you don't consciously work at it.[5]

Visual language provides a tool to build an image of an organization's goals that can be displayed widely. The image is constructed by people within the organization and it helps them convince others to share their goal and work toward it on a high-priority basis. This shared commitment defeats the time-slips-away problem and leads to results.

At the end of a visual communication session, the group's work product, the image or map, provides a long-standing visual reference to the work of the group.

- We can see how the whole fits together.

- We can break the patterns of how we have looked at our world and interpreted the information available.

- We can remove the overriding hierarchy because the maps show process flows.

- We can see the intellectual logic of the situation and the emotional drivers and restraints.

- We can see ourselves in the map and walk around in it.

- We can tell stories around it where we are the heroes.

- We can draw from it the power to stop looking outside ourselves for magic solutions.

The symbols become our common vocabulary. Those of us who remember facts best will find them there. Those who remember feelings will find them and those who remember distilled, summary ideas will also find them.

The map becomes the "Rosetta stone" between our intellectual selves and our emotional selves and between those of us who are analytical and those who are intuitive.[6] In the map we will have made images of and given names to our problems, our aspirations, and our commitments. This puts us at ease with ourselves and within our group and allows us to focus on the work of the organization calmly and confidently.

The visual language foundation principles encourage us to involve the right people; employ our visual capability; free ourselves from the constraints of experience without losing the benefits; open our youthful, creative spirits; and unite in purpose with our colleagues. Each principle is a small force for increased effectiveness but together they become a powerful force that can help us overcome personal prisons and organization overcast.

Chapters 6 and 7 show how visual languages work and provide some applied examples.

SECTION III

HOW TO USE VISUAL LANGUAGES

HOW VISUAL LANGUAGES WORK

Now that we've explored *what* visual languages can accomplish and *why* they work, this chapter will look in more depth at *how* they work.

JUST BY BEING AVAILABLE

The visual language starts working for you just by its existence and your knowledge of it. If, as a single individual, you face the need to clarify, solve, or communicate about an issue, the language gives you a tool to take your ideas and feelings and build a powerful message. If you have responsibilities in a group and know that the visual language can help you quickly achieve consensus, you won't sit on complex issues until they have become serious problems or lost opportunities. In both cases, the visual language helps you make your issue mind-sized and moves you toward action.

WORKSHOP PLANNING

As organizations have become flatter, more people and groups tend to be involved with issues and there is seldom a single authority who can make a decision. Solving a complex problem with a group session may take from a few hours to two days. This is a considerable investment and requires careful planning. Just the act of planning starts the process of making the issue mind-sized.

First, the issue has to be defined by answering these questions. Just what is the problem? What business objectives do we have? Who "owns" the problem and should sponsor the effort to solve it? Is it urgent and important enough for the investment of effort?

Then, the scope is discussed. What groups are involved? Who are the stakeholders? Who should participate in the workshop? Do they know the details? Do they have the respect of their peers? Do they have the power to implement an agreed solution? As the scope grows, so does the complexity. The stakes get higher and the bar is raised.

Take, for example, the case of a multidivision company that was determined to improve its customer service. The corporation decided that the route to world-class customer service was to name a functional excellence manager for customer service. Cindy Shamansky's measures included increased overall customer satisfaction ratings, reduced redundancy of effort, and reduced operating costs. However, each division had its own customer service structure and methods and ideas for improvement and, after several months on the job, she was making no headway either in meeting her measured objectives or in forming a receptive atmosphere for future progress.

When Cindy heard about visual language's capabilities to help communication and creative thinking, she decided to try it. She brought together three divisional representatives who were sympathetic to the overall corporate objectives and started to talk out the problem. As they discussed the difficulty of reconciling the views of all of the divisions, Cindy started to see her problem not as one of convincing people to change but rather one of creating a shared vision of an ideal customer service function that all divisions could strive for. The payoff would be world-class customer service, but it would be built on

- The expertise of each of the divisions
- Teamwork that could be developed between divisions
- Respect for company values
- Excellent communication with others

Cindy and her associates drew up a list of people who had a major stake in the customer service process. Cindy included each of the divisional managers and key representatives of the information systems function. She established the scope as being all businesses in the corporation and invited 16 people, including herself.

Following sound practice for planning and business process redesign, she decided that the sequence of events should be

1. Understand and agree about today's operation.

2. Agree on a vision of an ideal.

3. Set transition strategies and agree on an action plan.[1]

This meant building three different maps. Each would take about a half day. The overall group would be broken into four subgroups that would each build a map showing their views in one and one-half to two hours. Then, each of the four subgroups would present its map to the others. When the presentations were all completed, they would discuss their differing perspectives and try to agree about what one single composite map would look like.

The company's current operation would be addressed on the morning of the first day, the ideal would follow that afternoon, and the strategies would be worked on the next morning. This was very ambitious, but Cindy hoped that the time pressure would be a help rather than a problem.

This planning helped Cindy come to grips with her problem and start a process that could lead to a solution.

THE SYMBOLS AND MAP BUILDING

Addressing the first step of the change process, understanding how customer service works today, requires a language that can show a process where many events may be occurring simultaneously. Cindy decided to use the village mapping language for this, where a building represents a group or a function and roads represent interconnections. It made sense to her that the ideal state of customer service also be shown as a village.

She introduced the workshop session objectives and broke the attendees into four subgroups as planned. She showed them the dictionary of symbols, introduced the mechanics of the language, and set them to their task.

Building a village map is a process with six major elements. Although it is described as a sequence of steps, it is really iterative. That is, the execution of each element may lead to the modification of elements previously worked on.

Step 1. Structure of the Situation

In the first step, the group members decide what functions or buildings constitute the process being mapped. They identify them by writing signposts for each and placing them on the green background. If a building is somehow isolated from the others, it is placed on a hillside.

This initial step challenges the map builders to identify all the players in the process. It provides a context for all the evaluations that follow and thereby adds perspective to any disagreements. All those in a sub-group need to agree on the selection and placement of symbols.

The completed first step of one of the maps looked like Figure 6.1.

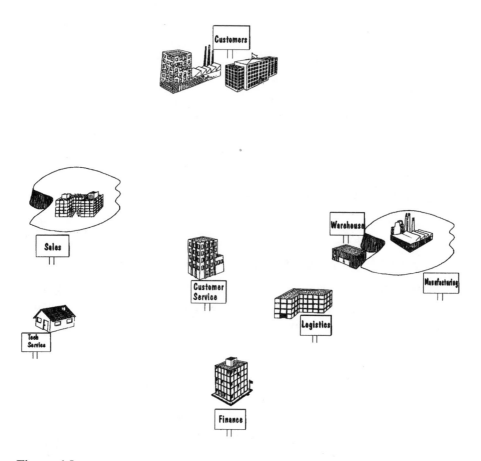

Figure 6.1

Step 2. Communications

The interconnections of the functions are then shown by placing roads between the buildings. The quality of the connection is shown by the nature of the road symbol selected. The information passed is identified by writing on an envelope. (This step frequently leads to the discovery that some buildings have been left out of the first step!)

At the end of step 2, the map looked as in Figure 6.2.

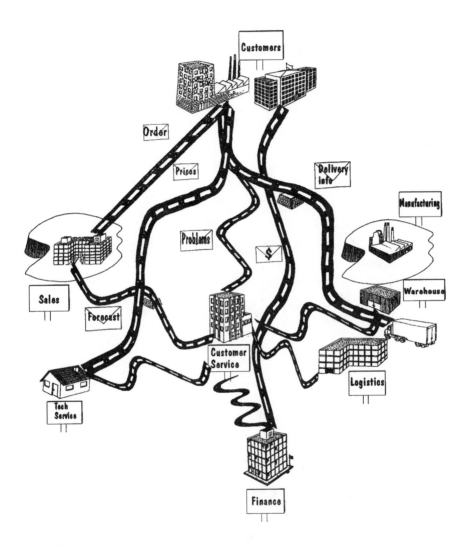

Figure 6.2

Step 3. Obstacles to Communication/Problems

Particular problems with the information flow and overall process are discussed, the group chooses an appropriate symbol to represent them, and adds them to the map along with an explanatory signpost.

Some of the problem symbols Cindy's group used are

- Berlin wall: A deliberately built barrier.

- Golfers: Informal contacts or decisions made but not communicated.

- Sheep on the road: An accepted but dysfunctional conflict of priorities.

- Crowns: A symbol that one function is regarded as having higher value than another.

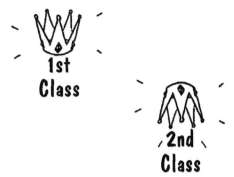

Step 4. Environment

When step 3 is finished and the main activities have all been represented and evaluated, any elements in the environment that have not already been shown are now addressed. This includes any specific ones and the more hidden paradigms.

When the map is complete, the group members look at it and ask themselves if it

- Represents all significant parts of the process in question. Significance is relative. Maps can be constructed for different levels of detail. In fact, one of the advantages of the mapping metaphor is that in most circumstances the participants understand that it may be necessary to build maps which allow you to "pop up" to a larger-scale map or "drop down" to a smaller-scale map to address different parts of the issue at hand.

- Feels balanced, with the problems shown in proper perspective.

- Includes all their ideas.

Step 5. Check

When they feel the map is complete, the builders should stand back from their creation and perform an overall check. They need to first make sure that the map's logic is correct. Checking logic visually is easier than using text but still should be done methodically, reviewing stakeholders, communications, and environmental and qualitative factors. The second step is to make sure that its visual/emotional messages are correct. Does it feel right? Are things that bad? Or that good? Do the qualitative symbols properly reflect the magnitude of the problem and give a clear sense of priority?

Step 6. Narrative

The final task for the map builders is to write a brief narrative to record the most important points and ensure that the map's main messages would be clear to an outside observer. Any agreed priorities of problems or reflections about their root causes may be recorded. It is possible to write the narrative as the map is being built if the mapping team is large or includes a word-oriented person. The whole team should review and agree with the narrative.

The final map of the current state of Cindy's customer service, Figure 6.3, shows difficult communications throughout the process. The message is passed visually through the symbols, and key points are noted in the narrative box on the bottom right.

PHYSICAL ACTIVITIES AND HELPING PATTERNS

As each subgroup builds its map, the people sit, stand, gesture, move their chairs around, walk, eat snacks, and take coffee or other drinks when they want. They move from small groups to the full group and back to small groups. These kinds of movements, and the manual activities involved in using the visual symbols, make the body much more physically active than in a typical meeting. They engage the participants more fully in the process and the participants are able to send messages to their colleagues by their body movements.

Suspending the behavior constraints of a formal meeting carries over into the thinking process and encourages it to be more spontaneous. For example, when you stand next to your colleague facing your map as you build it, you face the problem together. You discuss the symbol in front of you and the individual who proposed the ideas it represents is less exposed to evaluation. You build together rather than attack each other.

The physical freedom of this workshop setting invites you to relate to people as the individuals they are, not just as representatives of their organizations. You ask each other for help, such as, "Would you look up this symbol in the dictionary?" or "Could you write that sign for me?" You bring somebody a coffee. These small acts build a sense of community and belonging. The succession of small, successful inter-working activities establishes a foundation on which trust can develop.

PRESENTATIONS AND CONSENSUS BUILDING

When the maps are completed, they are presented individually to the whole group. Each presenter describes the process as shown on his or

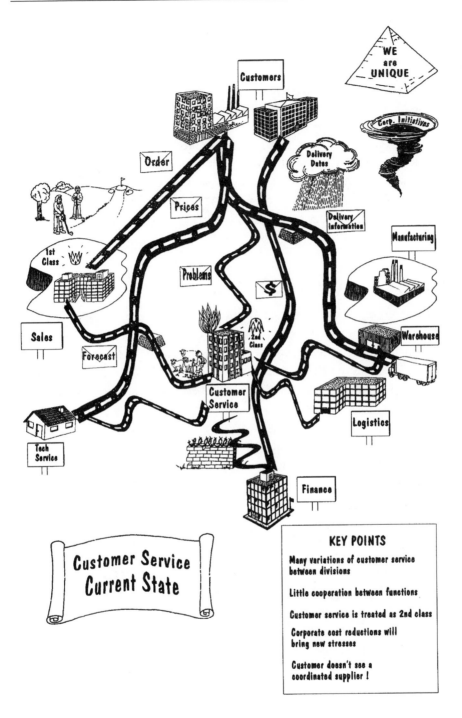

Figure 6.3

her map in only a few minutes. No questions are allowed until all the presentations are completed. In Cindy's case, she commented that all the maps looked different and asked the group members to identify points where they agreed. She focused the discussion on identifying the best ideas from each map and building a new, consolidated map that reflected the consensus view.

The group members highly appreciated the presentations, said that they learned a lot from their colleagues, and were astonished at how quickly they had been able to get to the heart of the issue. Because the group discussion was focused on building a common map from the products of the subgroups, it further encouraged constructive interworking.

THE IDEAL VISION

After the group members had built and agreed on a map of today's operation, Cindy moved them to phase 2 of the change process, building a map of how they ideally would like the customer service function to work. Her charge to the group was: "Build a map that shows how the process will work once we have fully satisfied our customer at the lowest possible cost. Don't worry about how to get there. One thing each of you should do is think about how you believe the environment will change in the future and what values you think should guide us.

"Close your eyes for a moment. Imagine how things will work two years from now when we've overcome all of our current problems, when our activities are guided by our values and we've met our objectives. Run with your ideas, however wild. You probably can't build the perfect map in your small group, but if we take all the best ideas together, we can create the ideal vision."

Cindy reorganized the subgroups so that everybody was working with different people. She thought that this would further increase participation for any people who may have been dominated by the personality of somebody else in their subgroup, and she hoped it would help build new relationships and stimulate fresh thinking. The vocabulary of symbols was the same as with the first map except that a blue sky symbol was added to the top of the map. The completed map is shown in Figure 6.4.

Each group had thought about company values somewhat differently, but everyone agreed that an ideal process would have to be much simpler than the current process. The customer deserved more respect and discipline from the company.

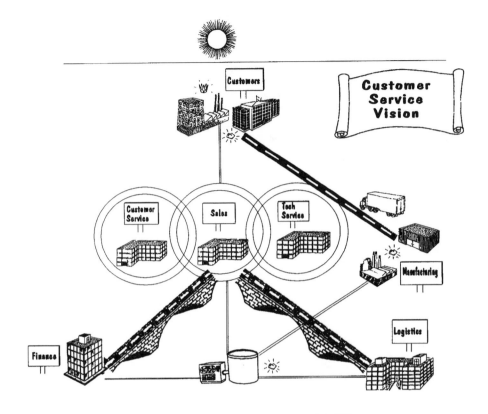

VISION COMPONENTS

1. CUSTOMER SERVICE IS A CRITICAL BUSINESS STRATEGY.

2. ONE FACE IS PRESENTED TO THE CUSTOMER - GLOBALLY.

3. CUSTOMER SERVICE PEOPLE ARE PROFESSIONALS WITH ESTABLISHED CAREER PATHS AND TRAINING AND DEVELOPMENT PROGRAMS.

4. SYNERGIES AMONG CUSTOMER SERVICE DEPARTMENTS ARE EXPLOITED.

5. REAL-TIME SUPPLY AND ORDER SYSTEMS ARE USED FOR MANAGEMENT DECISIONS.

Figure 6.4

The dominant image in the combined map is the global partnership of technical services, sales, and customer service. They are all on an equal level, share the same information systems, and present a coordinated face to the customer. This paradigm shift from independent entities on hillsides to tightly linked functions sprang from the group's emotional reaction to the discordant image they built of the current state and their feelings that this was no way to treat their customers.

CREATIVITY AND VISUAL PERCEPTION

We can better understand how Cindy's and other groups have been able to use visual language to make paradigm shifts and solve complex problems by considering the observations of noted art professor Betty Edwards. She believes that images can take on and convey meanings that are beyond the power of words to express. They can help us synthesize diverse sensory impressions and intellectual ideas. The complex functioning we experience when we look at images seems simple because we already possess competence in visual language and perceptual thought. Visual memory, analysis, and integration are already part of our internal wiring.

To show how visual language can lead to creative problem solving, Edwards starts with psychologist Jacob Getzels' five-step model of creativity.[2]

1	2	3	4	5
First insight	Saturate	Incubate	Illuminate	Verify
			*	
			The	
			"ah-ha"	

Edwards postulates that the left- and right-brain hemispheres naturally dominate at different stages of the creative process. The right side is the main actor in achieving the first insight, perhaps in response to consciously posed questions. The left side naturally dominates the saturation phase by researching, categorizing, and analyzing. The intuitive, perceptual pattern-seeking right brain is responsible for the incubation stage and illumination. The left hemisphere fully controls the verification step. Because the left hemisphere tends to dominate the right, many people attempt to work through the entire process of problem solving with analytical methods, and this yields unsatisfactory results.

Edwards has found, through her work and teaching, that drawing can help relieve excessive left hemisphere dominance and improve our creative capacity by accessing and applying our emotions and intuitions throughout the first four stages. If, for example, we apply our right brain and emotions as well as our intellectual research during the saturation phase, we gain access to a new, rich set of material for use during idea incubation.

When groups use visual symbols to build maps, they are in effect drawing an image. In Cindy's example and others that have been described, the groups put their thoughts and feelings about the current state of their issue into a visual form by building a map. In doing this, they were applying their right hemisphere capabilities and recording their emotions. Because their maps made order out of the various factors, the left brain was better able to work on that information and also advance the creative process.

The map building thus provided high-quality input for both hemispheres processing in the later saturation and incubation phases. Keeping the images in front of, or available to, the group is one of the reasons that map-building sessions can be so efficient and move a group from first insight through illumination and well into verification.

TRANSITION PLAN

For phase 3 of the change process, transition planning, Cindy wanted to continue using the resources of the entire group. She had seen too many individual staff planners go off to develop pristine flowcharts in great detail that were of little value after the project met the delays, problems, interpersonal complexity, and compromises of the real world. She wanted the group to use the map to contribute members' experience and intuition to showing what was the best route to take and what were the pitfalls to implementing the vision.

She chose the river mapping language for this because she wanted a metaphor that would graphically show the passage of time. The river itself shows time and Cindy was happy knowing that there were no rivers as straight as the lines on flowcharts.

The river map building process aims to make certain that map builders' analytical and emotional resources are both applied and are in harmony. It alternately moves them from analytical thinking to visual thinking and back again to ensure that all assumptions and paradigms are challenged, variables and possible routes are considered, and that the resulting plan is realistic.

Step 1. Construct the Streams of Action

You start the map-building process by listing all the actions needed to achieve the objective, organizing them into logical groupings, and then showing them in time sequence along rivers. The only difference from traditional planning approaches here is that you discuss the actions before writing them down. This is a logical, analytical, intellectual process.

The first step of a map to implement Cindy's customer service vision is shown in Figure 6.5.

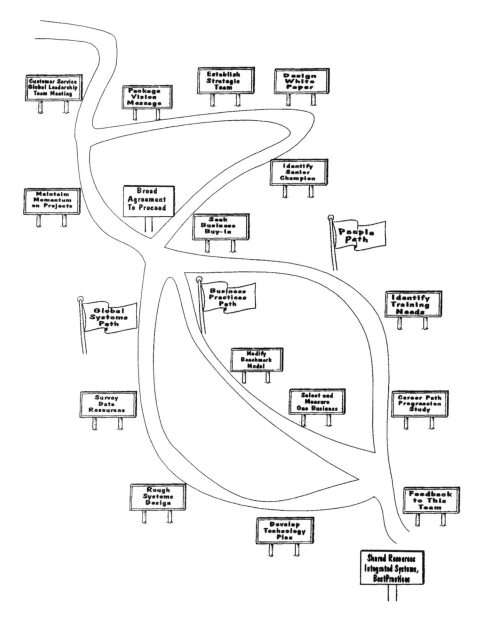

Figure 6.5

Step 2. Landscape the Streams of Action: Animate the Actions and Show Obstacles/Risks/Help

After the skeleton of the river map has been built, you animate the action step signs with visual symbols wherever possible. This characterization gives them a face as well as a name and begins the process of stimulating your imagination about what can go wrong, what will be your obstacles, and what unintended outcomes could await you. It starts to employ your emotional resources and intuition in addition to your logic.

You want the map to put the transition into perspective. How much work will it be? Where will there be problems? How serious are the risks? When you identify an obstacle, you then have to decide on an image to characterize it. This gives it weight and priority. Obstacles, such as a tree fallen across the river, often require that an alternative stream be taken. In such a case, the specific action needed to circumvent the barrier is shown on the alternate stream. Some obstacles, such as a sandbar in the river, do not require an alternate route and the action or help needed to overcome it may be noted alongside. The need for help is often overlooked in strategy planning. The map created at the end of step 2 is shown in Figure 6.6.

Step 3. Decide How to Show Responsibilities and Controls

After looking at the obstacles, controls have more meaning. You can insert checkpoints, milestones, and target dates in a way that gage progress but also make you conscious of the risks that remain. You can show responsibilities for individual actions or entire strategies with the riverboat and hat symbols.

Step 4: Make Intuitive and Analytical Checks

After you think the map is complete, you can do three further things to ensure its quality. First, review the full vocabulary of symbols to see if it stimulates you to think about anything related to the success of the project that you've overlooked.

Second, evaluate the overall appearance of the map. Does it give the right visual messages? Is the concentration of activity in certain areas representative of the amount of work to be done? Are the options available and decisions to be taken visible? Are the risks realistic? Does the map make emotional sense and does the feeling of risk or simplicity it gives correspond to the group's intuition?

Third, without referencing the symbols, look analytically at the signs and follow the river branches sequentially. Is anything important missing? Is the map logical?

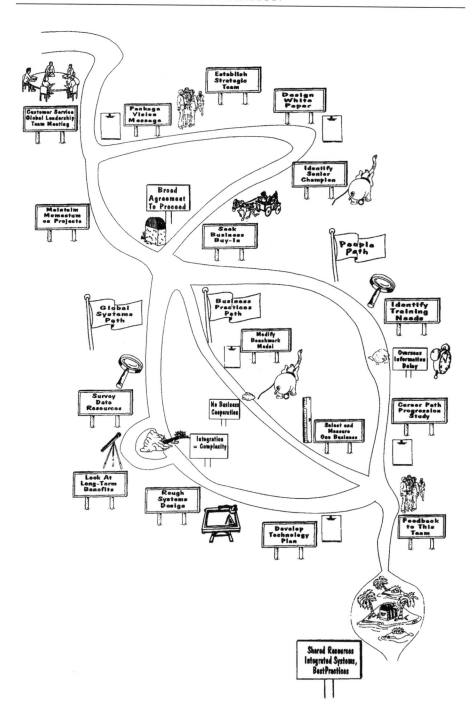

Figure 6.6

Step 5. Write a Narrative

As a final step, write down the key points made in the map. The map and narrative together should explain clearly all the key messages you want to convey to a reader.

Cindy's completed map is shown in Figure 6.7.

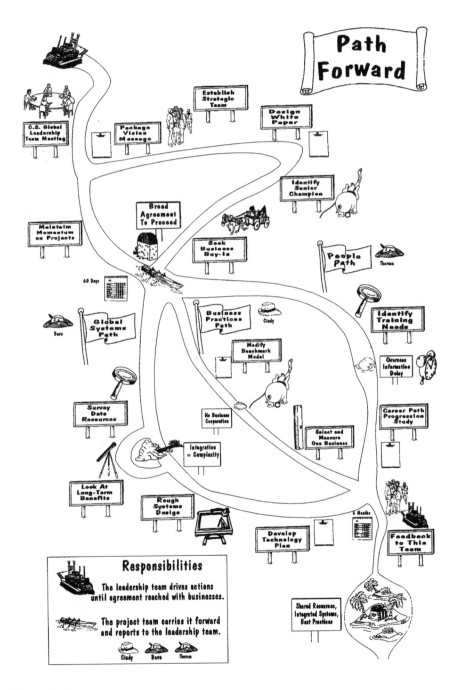

Figure 6.7

DISPLAYING THE MAPS

Cindy and others used the maps in many presentations, gained buy in of the business leaders, and are progressing on implementation. By displaying the maps on their office walls, each group member made a public statement about his or her assessment and intent and stimulated discussions on details.

The foundation principles built into the language and its group processes can be seen at work in Cindy's example. Simply by scheduling a workshop of the stakeholders to try to make the problem mind-sized, Cindy started using them. With the symbols, the group members put their child to work telling picture stories with both words and images and put clarity before purity. They anchored their analysis and the challenge of their task raised the bar. Building the maps helped them build a team and gave them a map to steer by.

Visual languages can make it easy and natural to follow principles that improve organization effectiveness. Chapter 7 shows a set of examples of where visual languages have been applied and generated significant benefits.

TOOLS FOR RENEWAL:
A SET OF EXAMPLES

Many capable people are frustrated today. They work for highly regarded companies but, although they are supposed to be empowered, it is harder than ever to accomplish tasks that involve others and require change. There are so many agreements, buy ins, nonobjections, and other hurdles to jump that they run out of energy and drive. Big organizations have reduced the layers of structure that need to approve decisions but the number of people involved in the process has tended to increase. Because the new lean, flat structures don't have new management processes and their people don't have new skills of interworking, many are no more effective than their predecessors.

Visual languages can be used to build new communication and decision-making processes for flat organizations. A critical asset they bring is speed: speed of understanding, speed of formulating objectives and plans, speed of consensus, and speed of implementation. They also bring efficiency because they help people communicate and work together as teams. Speed and efficiency are critical because, where companies are lean and power is close to the operating level, decision makers cannot afford to take much time away from their jobs.

Visual languages can help solve problems and set direction even when authority is dispersed and no specific goals have been set. They can liberate the vitality of entrepreneurial employees and help build a dynamic team spirit to make a lean organization truly formidable.

Lean, flat organizations have no time for fretting, NIH, slip-sliding, and other syndromes that hold back traditional hierarchies. They need a new marching rhythm. They need the rhythm of stakeholders in processes coming together when needed to set the direction by consensus and then returning to their jobs. What they need is a rhythm like that of the minutemen of the American Revolutionary War era. They were hands-on farmers and workers. The community had neither the money nor the desire to support a standing army, but when a community need arose, the minutemen assembled quickly, met the challenge, and returned just as quickly to their farms and jobs. The towns of colonial New England were governed in a similar way. There was no standing government. The people in the community would come together for town meetings whenever the need arose, democratically solve the issue, and return to their business.

Anyone who can bring together the stakeholders in their issue, make it mind-sized, and develop a consensus plan to solve it, will not be frustrated but will be challenged.

This chapter is comprised of a series of examples showing how visual languages have helped solve problems and helped organizations renew themselves.

1. Reengineering a supply chain

2. Government downsizing

3. Organization restructuring

4. Transatlantic supply chain coordination

5. Merchandising plan

6. Facilities management

7. Public administration program planning

8. Strategic information systems planning

Examples 1 and 2 describe workshops that had a profound impact on their respective organizations and are covered in detail. The six other examples have shorter descriptions of their issues, stakeholders, the role of visual language, and the results and benefits. The reader wanting to focus on specific types of examples may wish to reference the table of visual language application examples in the front of the book, which lists all the book's examples by function and type of benefit achieved.

Example 1. Reengineering a Supply Chain

This first example shows how the minuteman approach worked successfully at a multinational company. In late 1992, Joe Slater had just been appointed to be the company's global supply chain manager. His boss, Charlie Crew, was the new manager of integrated operations for the business. Although the business had operations and customers around the world, it was being run on a country or regional basis. Joe and Charlie's mission was to turn the business into an integrated, global operation, yielding both better customer service and lower costs. Integrated operations implied major changes in the way the business functioned, changes in jobs, new demands for information, and new decision-making processes.

The task was immense and Joe expected many obstacles. The worldwide business team of about 40 executives would have to agree on a new vision of how the business would work. They'd have to understand how customers would be serviced, how orders would be handled, what plants would supply what customers, how forecasts would be made, how logistics would be handled, how the new responsibilities would be split, and how the operation would be staffed.

Joe's first step was to team up with Toni Skipper, the quality manager for the division. Together they planned an approach. They both felt that the scale of the task was a major challenge and were concerned about how to structure a session where dozens of people who knew the details of the operation could perform effective analysis and make good decisions.

Joe had some experience with visual languages in his previous job as the business's supply chain manager for Europe. The company's global language was English, but its European staff had varying ability to speak and work in English on complex issues. The visual symbols gave everyone a common language and helped make sure that ideas were accurately represented.

Joe commented, "By involving the stakeholders, you get a practical look at the issue, not an ivory tower approach. Besides, its the people who do the job who are going to have to make any changes, so if it's their idea, it gets done fast and everybody is better off.

"I learned this lesson when I wanted to get a computer application changed by the end of the year. It was June and I knew that if I could get the project done by December, the business would save $2 million.

I closed my door and worked like crazy for three days to draw up a very precise plan on how we could do it. My flowchart covered half of my wall. The problem was, when I brought in some of the key people to talk over how we could do it, they'd look at the chart, their eyes would glaze over, and they'd kind of sleepwalk out of my office.

"I guess I'm a slow learner, but after this happened three or four times, I knew my great idea was going nowhere. I changed approaches and brought together the order entry supervisor, the information systems manager, the customer service manager, and a half dozen other people who were key to making this project a success. I explained the payoff if the system could be changed by year end, but I didn't dare bring out my chart. I just asked them if they would use this visual language for a couple of hours to work out if it would be possible.

"Well, it was just the most amazing thing. I split them up into three groups and they came back together in two hours. They all said there were some risks but that it could be done. They showed each other the maps they had built, talked through some ideas, and that was that. I didn't say anything when I noticed that, although their maps looked different and seemed to be relatively simple, they said almost exactly what I had shown on my big flowchart. Anyway, we got the job done and saved the money.

"That was in Europe, but Toni and I decided to use a similar approach here. We needed to involve a lot of people and we didn't want just to restructure things. We wanted to get people to think globally, to think in terms of processes and not organizations, and to really have value for continuous improvement."

Toni, Joe, and Charlie foresaw a two-step change process. The first step would be to bring together the top business managers and a number of highly respected functional specialists. The objective was to develop a common understanding about what integrated operations meant and, in general, how they would work. As a second step, Toni, Joe, and Charlie would bring together a more operational-level group that would look in detail at the current global supply chains and build a vision and plan that would tie in with the overall business vision.

The first workshop was very productive. Toni observed, "When we started, I'm sure that there weren't two people in the room who would have given you the same answer if you asked what integrated operations was. They would have been even farther apart if you had asked what it would mean to them. Frankly, we didn't think we could work all the way through this issue in two days, but that was all the time we could get.

"We had a very diverse group, covering about all the functions in the business, three of our global regions, and four levels of hierarchy, so we expected problems in understanding. Our people are very independent, so we also expected vocal challenges to any new directions that would be proposed.

"Fortunately, none of those things happened. The visual language surprised people at first but they got down to business in a hurry. We were amazed that, by noon on the first day, we all agreed on why things weren't working well. Actually, most of us learned a lot more from that half day than we would like to admit. The session to create a vision also went very well, with some surprising new ideas that got sold on the spot!

Joe introduced the second session the following week and explained in only the most general terms the direction that the leadership group had agreed upon. He did not show the first group's maps. He told the group members that their challenge was to look in detail at the supply chain and propose the best possible operation. Then they would see if it fit into management's framework. In two days, the participants developed their plan in detail. Their maps showed a new set of improvement ideas that they prepared to implement. Fortunately, there was a good fit with management's overall plan.

"It became clear that we'd made the mistake of not inviting anybody from sales and marketing," said Toni. "We thought the general management could fill in for sales and marketing, but when we saw the number of interconnections involved, we knew that sales needed to buy in to the vision if it was to work." Toni had difficulty in scheduling all the key salespeople for a third session, and this posed a problem. If the operations integration effort was to proceed without sales, there would be an ongoing possibility of discord but, if it was to wait months, it would lose momentum. The only near opportunity was to have four hours at the end of a sales meeting coming the next month, and Toni decided to go for it. Neither she nor Joe was sure that the group could reach a sales operations vision in four hours, but it was worth a try.

The business director introduced the subject while the group ate lunch at a conference table. He challenged them to contribute all they could in the short time available and build maps that "tell it like it is." The salespeople had a lot of fun but were very quick to map out their current operation and its problems. They went on to develop their ideas on how they could better integrate and meet their customer needs and reached a consensus, just as several of them left to catch airplanes. The team was elated with its progress.

Charlie commented on the overall operations integration planning: "I have had plenty of experience trying to get things done in big companies and I have to admit I thought we were not leaving enough time to deal with these complex issues. Particularly in planning the first workshop, I thought we were setting our sights too high. I was proved wrong, though, and I'm glad of it.

"We have a lot of momentum now. Our vision of integrated operations has been built by more than 60 people and it is solid. The people who are implementing it are completely clear on what they're doing and why. Believe me, that's quite an accomplishment. You know, I like it when people mention when talking in the hallway that something is a crocodile and something else is a sandbar. It means that they're part of the team and their enthusiasm is high."

This example shows how a business can make sweeping changes with a sequence of interconnected planning sessions. The business not only set a new course, but also remade parts of its culture and improved the efficiency of its operation. Because the company fully involved key process stakeholders in direction setting, it is carrying out the transition with enthusiasm. And, the employees did it with only a small amount of time away from their line duties. This is a renewed organization following a new rhythm.

Example 2. Government Downsizing

Situation/Issue

When many different change processes need to be initiated at the same time, and when the success of one will influence the success of another, it is of vital importance to have excellent communication, efficiency, and alignment. The World Bank's principal institutional development specialist was faced with such a challenge as he advised the secretary to cabinet of an underdeveloped country about how the country could go about reforming the operations of all of its cabinet ministries or agencies.

The World Bank and the International Monetary Fund had insisted on important reductions in the cost of government operations as a precondition for loans that would help this new democracy gain fiscal stability. The newly elected leaders had run on a platform of better service and more accountability in government and agreed with the Bank's objective, but the question was how to accomplish it without creating economic chaos.

The stakes in managing the change process were high. Loss of confidence by aid agencies would cost the government needed financial resources, and loss of public support would increase the risk of labor union resistance and loss of momentum. The specialist and the secretary to cabinet discussed how to proceed and decided that the 50 top civil servants and a group of donor representatives and functional specialists would need to be brought together if a satisfactory plan was to be developed. They were certain that it would take a week to cover all the issues and that they would be lucky to succeed. They were concerned about the

- Need for a way to encourage government officials and donor agencies to understand the nature and depth of today's problems

- Need to stimulate fresh thinking about how to change 20-year-old bureaucratic approaches

- Problems of managing a very large group of people with different cultural and national backgrounds and widely differing objectives and experiences

- Need to hold participants' interest and enthusiasm through a long and complex analysis and avoid the deadening effect of speech after speech

Stakeholders

Some of the stakeholders in this broad change process included

- Permanent secretaries who run the various government agencies. In the previous government the incumbents were subject to regular change, apparently unrelated to performance. The new democratic government now told the permanent secretaries, "You are accountable to the people through the parliament. Reexamine your functions, improve the quality of service, and reduce costs." The permanent secretaries knew that this was an enormous challenge because policies and procedures were not in place and morale in their organizations was low.

- Local administrators were accountable to the local electorate, but controlled very few resources. They wanted the authority and means to fulfill their obligations.

- Labor unions were stakeholders because the government owned and operated a wide number of businesses due to the policies of the previous socialist government. They were not invited to the first strategy-setting session but would be invited to later ones. They had made it clear that they would paralyze the country with strikes if their members were not treated fairly.

- Elected officials knew that success of this reform would bear heavily on whether the move to democracy would endure.

- World Bank representatives wanted the government to conceive a plan that could reduce government dominance of the economy without causing political disruption.

- The British Overseas Development Administration had been working for years to help upgrade the quality of government administration, particularly in local communities. It understood the need for real commitment by government officials and hoped for a plan that would distribute power in a balanced manner.

Role of Visual Language

The institutional specialist decided that a visual language offered the best chance of success on such an ambitious undertaking. He involved a local meeting facilitator and a visual language specialist and they planned out an intensive four-day meeting. He knew that each government agency needed to make its own unique changes but that all the agencies needed to agree on a number of common points.

1. How the government should decentralize authority

2. How planning, budgeting, and financial control should be improved

3. How to improve personnel performance and redesign the reward system

4. A layoff policy

The workshop was brought to order by the deputy secretary to the cabinet, who outlined the challenges facing the government. The group was broken into nine subgroups of five or six which focused on one of the four key processes of government listed previously. The subgroups built visual models of the processes, compared their views in plenary sessions, and reached full consensus on all consequent matters. Their sequence of analysis followed the proven quality improvement method of examining the current state, projecting an ideal vision, and creating a transition plan. In addition, they defined terms of reference for leaders of change in individual agencies and the overall program coordinator.

The workshop was highly participative and everyone had the opportunity to thoroughly voice opinions and help build the plan.

Results/Benefits

The maps of the present state provided an opportunity for catharsis, where the government employees could air their grievances about the former government and pronounce their willingness to change.

While making the second maps, the group generated fresh ideas, most notably for the intractable problem of how to move thousands of people out of government jobs without creating disastrous unemployment. The transition maps gave participants the opportunity to make commitments to change actions. Because donor agencies came to more clearly understand the local political situation, they were able to see how they could contribute to the reform process.

Constructing the maps provided a springboard for mutual understanding, and teamwork reached unprecedented high levels. Donor agency people had the opportunity to solve problems with people whom they had once monitored and controlled and they were struck by their competency. Government officials got to know and respect the donors as people and respect the personal contributions they could make to thinking through and solving problems. The relationship paradigm between the international agencies and the government changed, at least for a time, from donor–recipient to partnership in problem solving. The results exceeded all the objectives the stakeholders had set and established a firm plan for reform.

Change, One Problem at a Time

Change does not often come in the major programs described in the previous two examples. More often, it comes in less apparent, more confined steps. Single successes have a way of snowballing toward renewal. They can open up your vistas about the kind of fresh thinking and speed that are possible, whether you are in industry, service organizations, government, university administration, health services, or international organizations. While visual languages are excellent for solving the most complex problems, they also can be applied to a wide range of individual business problems and start the renewal process from smaller seeds.

Example 3. Organization Restructuring

Situation/Issue

The director of a corporate service department, who had more than 1000 people spread over 20 locations, needed to refocus and reduce his staff. The department's three main functions (customer service, information systems, and logistics support services) were critical to customer satisfaction, but competitive pressures in the market required reducing the corporation's overall product cost structure.

The director was convinced that wide participation in the change process was the key to understanding changing customer requirements, generating fresh ideas about how to reduce costs, and gaining commitment to whatever changes would be made.

During the course of six months, he had brought the top 25 managers together twice for three-day meetings to discuss how to refocus the department's functions and try to crystallize the tough downsizing issues that were facing the department. These meetings had yielded very little. The issues remained vague and it was becoming evident that the group members were avoiding clarity because it would lead to changes that would cost some of them their jobs. Pressure was building on the director, and he was aware that if he didn't take action soon, the business managers who were his customers would force him to make changes by executive decision.

Stakeholders

The organization included three levels for each of the three functions: field operations, field staff, and central staff. Some of the important differences in view that were holding back progress were

- The three function managers disagreed on how dramatic the changes should be. One wanted to eliminate the function managers' jobs and decentralize, another wanted to eliminate the field staff level, and another wanted to leave things alone and just help the internal customers better appreciate the value they added to products sold.

- Central customer service staff were convinced that the most efficient structure required a few central specialists to define optimum methods with local, on-site staff to carry out the day-to-day tasks.

- Central information systems staff members were confident in their abilities and felt that it was obvious that, if there were to be any changes, they should increase in size and extend their authority over the less capable local groups.

- Ex-central functional staff members felt that central ties were superfluous and wasted time and resources. Redundancy in their own ranks was obvious to them, but they liked and respected each other and preferred to aim improvement ideas elsewhere.

- Line supervisors in the field saw an unhealthy split in the organization between thinkers and doers. They thought the central staff was out of touch with real customer needs and that sites were being starved of resources in critical areas.

Role of Visual Language

To resolve the organization dilemma, vastly differing points of view had to be reconciled and creative solutions found. Time was now of the essence. To reconcile these different points of view and find a creative solution, a visual symbol language workshop was convened for the 25 managers.

Results/Benefits

Most participants came to the workshop armed with new organization structures to propose. But, rather than allowing the discussion to focus on comparisons of structures, the director asked the participants to study the department's function and underlying processes, both from a customer view and a service provider view. When an ideal view of the processes was agreed upon, the natural organization structure and relative sizing became evident to all. The group members decided to support a bold shift of responsibilities without considering the impact on their own jobs. They focused on their organization's reason for existence and decided that the only valid roles of the central group were to extend functional excellence and to operate central facilities when it was more cost-effective to the corporation.

They decided that business units would have the right to take over and operate any of their three functions and be subject only to functional guidance from the central group. A path forward was charted that defined the way the change would be communicated and executed and the values that would be adhered to in staff redeployment and downsizing.

Within a few weeks from the end of the workshop, the restructuring was announced. Five of the workshop participants were reassigned to other duties, some businesses recruited staff out of the department, and some asked the department to operate functions for them. The change was smoothly made and resulted in significant cost savings. The new structure was used as a model for other central corporate groups.

Example 4. Transatlantic Supply Chain Coordination

Situation/Issue

The corporate supply chain manager of a petrochemicals company was concerned that transatlantic bulk materials handling was not operating at a high quality standard. A fragmented, product-oriented approach was being taken and there was a lack of understanding of equipment requirements. Customer service was erratic and the number of tank containers had grown more than 300 percent in the past two years.

The manager believed that not only were the total costs not visible but also that there was an exposure to safety incidents because there was no overall management/ownership for the function. While U.S.–Europe cooperation had been adequate on an operating level, relations were more cool on the planning and managerial level.

Stakeholders

There were three types of stakeholders.

- The U.S. logistics specialists and managers were fully knowledgeable in the technical aspects of bulk cargo shipment but saw their main duties as ending when ships left port.

- European logistics specialists knew their local situations but had avoided taking the time to get to know the people and problems on the U.S. side. Essential information often arrived after the material.

- The supply chain improvement project leader had some background in transatlantic issues and had been scheduled to look into the problem, but he was now being transferred to a new function. His replacement needed to meet the players and gain a firsthand understanding of the situation.

Role of Visual Language

A visual symbol language was selected as the vehicle for the two-day workshop of 15 people because the participants needed a view of the whole situation, had to keep focused on the problem, and had to avoid discussion diversions into other areas. Its teambuilding characteristics were also a major consideration.

Results/Benefits

The corporate and regional representatives from both sides of the Atlantic formed into a cohesive unit with mutual esteem and personal appreciation by the end of the session. Together they specified a new organization responsible for cost-effective global transport of bulk materials. Specifically, they agreed to plans for

- Improved customer service through better equipment availability, on-time delivery, and communications

- Improved control through a centralized system for data access, identifying technical expertise, and minimizing equipment needs

Because of the participation at the workshop, the corporate and regional representatives immediately achieved senior management approval for the resources and systems development expenses needed to make the recommended changes.

Savings have already started with a projected total of $5 million per year relating to operation of owned/leased equipment. Reduced capital costs will add further savings.

Perhaps the greatest benefit of all was the development of an action plan to reduce safety risks, including full coordination on equipment and fittings specifications, testing, and managed safety inspections. The success of this short, intense analysis inspired studies in related areas and wider improvements in safety and efficiency.

Example 5. Merchandising Plan

Situation/Issue

The general manager of a division of a diversified products company wanted to upgrade the image of an older industrial product and decrease customer sensitivity to price. Customer surveys showed that, although the product had once been a leader, there were now several products perceived to be of equal quality and better price on the market. This issue had been on and off agendas for two years. It wouldn't go away, but managers didn't want to take charge of addressing it because they thought it would drag them into never-ending discussions with no result.

Stakeholders

The internal stakeholders had no history of collaboration and were accustomed to being left alone, with an occasional directive from headquarters.

- The sales force had been selling the product for a long time and held the view that the product had become a commodity. The salespeople were comfortable selling to existing customers on a low margin. They felt that, if they made excessive claims for the product, they would lose credibility with their customers.

- Regional sales managers (who also were responsible for other products) believed that intensive efforts on this product would detract from sales of higher-margin products.

- Technical service personnel had other priorities and wanted to be sure of the company's overall commitment before gearing up the resources needed to promote new product applications.

- The marketing communications department felt it didn't have enough understanding to develop an effective campaign.

Role of Visual Language

The general manager decided to try a visual language workshop because he wanted people to think differently about the situation and generate new ideas. He also selected it for its efficiency because taking salespeople out of the field for staff assignments was discouraged. The workshop required only six hours.

Results/Benefits

While building its maps the group asked and answered questions, including

- How was the product promoted in the past?
- How were customers using it?
- Who was using it?
- Did it have other applications?

As the group members saw that they weren't fully exploiting the assets of the product's reputation and their accompanying strong technical service offering, the group started to convince itself that the product had enough residual leadership image to be worth the cost of trying to revive it.

The group members developed a process to merchandise the product and set an aggressive implementation plan using existing resources. They raised prices the next quarter, kept their market share in all sectors and even slightly increased it in others, and substantially increased margin. Prices have been maintained and cash flow from this business is moving toward previous highs.

A secondary, but important, result of this session was the realization that people could easily be brought in from the field to work on issues if the process made efficient use of their time. It brought about more participative decision making when the business addressed other problems.

Example 6. Facilities Management

Situation/Issue

The new director of corporate facilities management at a large conglomerate company was instructed by senior management to make major cost reductions.

Site managers had historically operated under the principle that "the tenant is king." They provided services and facilities as requested and paid by internal charges to the tenants. The new director's task was to understand the implications of the new cost reduction requirement, help the organization internalize it, and achieve the necessary savings while maintaining good tenant relations.

Stakeholders

There were two types of stakeholders.

- Tenants felt that, because they paid rent through internal charges, they had the right to make all key decisions about their facilities and services. Offices and facilities were generally only a small part of their total cost picture and they thought that a very comfortable work environment was a good means of achieving worker loyalty.

- The 12 major site facility managers had always been measured on the degree of customer satisfaction and avoided confrontation. They were not clear what the new corporate directive meant to them and, therefore, felt unable to act on it.

Role of Visual Language

The director was concerned that the facilities organization historically had been very hierarchy conscious and she wanted her 12 key staff members to take the lead in addressing this issue. Because it was so important, she also wanted to be involved, but she was concerned that her presence would make the key staff members hesitant to speak their minds or might encourage them to delegate decisions back to her.

She chose to convene a two-day visual language workshop because it created an environment where the group members could talk about new ideas without relying on her for answers and feeling that they shouldn't challenge her.

Results/Benefits

The role change had been very unsettling for the site managers, but the mapping helped them deal with their concerns and construct a new operating mode and a transition plan. They started by building maps of their current operation. The paradigm of tenant supremacy quickly became clear but some weaknesses and inefficiencies also became evident. As the site managers realized that there probably was a better way to operate the facilities function, they became more motivated to let go of the cozy relationships that characterized their present state. They saw that, by taking on greater responsibilities and confronting some tenants, they could save the company a lot of money.

In their maps of how they ideally wanted to operate, the group members proposed a new organization structure based on a new paradigm which reduced site autonomy. They then were able to identify a number of opportunities for consolidating facilities, hiring lower-cost contract operators, and restructuring their own assignments. Then they developed an action plan to communicate the new paradigm to facilities staff and tenants and to put in motion the cost-saving measures.

Several million dollars per year were realized from these measures. Tenants have not been uniformly happy about losing their autonomy, but they have accepted the new paradigm and day-to-day relationships have not been impaired.

By helping a group see its own role in the overall corporate picture, the visual language workshop allowed 12 people to become more productive contributors.

Example 7. Public Administration Program Planning

Situation/Issue

A health systems development specialist at the World Health Organization recognized that the ministry of health in a developing country had not been able to develop a unified plan and budget to address issues of critical importance to the health of the nation.

The extreme poverty of the country, a change in ministers, and the complexity of the task had led to an impasse where critical health services were not being provided to many communities. Rapid spread of the AIDS virus was a particular concern. Other international aid agencies had tried to help correct the paralysis of the central organization, but none had succeeded.

Stakeholders

The stakeholders had diverse interests.

- The new minister of health needed to create a unified plan of action for the ministry, change the top-heavy structure that she had inherited, and establish a viable budget in the shortest time possible.

- The directors of health service departments lacked self confidence and didn't feel able to set direction on these issues. They had only limited skills in strategic planning and general management. They needed to develop their own and their departments' internal management capabilities and better coordinate the central departments' actions with regions and districts.

- The directors of finance and human resources needed the health service directors to understand their requirements and follow them.

- The secretary of state took responsibility to coordinate the actions of the ministry with those of other ministries. He wanted to have a practical plan with realistic targets.

- Aid agency representatives were not in a position to set direction but wanted to understand the government's direction and priorities so that they could coordinate their programs with them.

- The health systems specialist wanted to help build efficiency in the ministry and ensure that technology and supplies were effectively delivered at regional hospitals and local health centers. He wanted them to develop strong planning skills that they could use in primary health care and in dealing with the spreading AIDS virus.

Role of Visual Language

The health systems specialist saw that he could contribute by organizing a session that would address health improvement planning combined with general management training. He decided to use a visual language for a number of reasons.

First, the stakeholders attending the workshop would have two different mother tongues: a native African dialect and Portuguese. However, the workshop would be conducted in French because everyone spoke French, including the aid agency representatives.

Second, the health systems specialist needed to ensure overall understanding, avoid overlaps, and generate personal commitment.

Third, he also hoped that the visual imagery would be a catalyst to help them solve the process problems that had defied their efforts.

Results/Benefits

The workshop fully succeeded. The group members identified root causes of a number of problems and agreed on the corrective actions needed. They developed a new organization structure, planned the necessary changes, and established the basis for the new budget. Most important, they could see what they had to do, strengthened their sense of purpose, and developed renewed enthusiasm for their tasks.

The specialist provided training in management and planning at three points during the week. He used the participants' maps for examples to demonstrate the concepts and, by relating the concepts directly to their individual problems, intensely focused the attention of the participants. The mapping process generated so much enthusiasm that the minister planned to use the maps as part of a national television broadcast, showing how health systems would be improved. His support added to participants' motivation to take improved work methods to the field.

Example 8. Strategic Information Systems Planning

Situation/Issue

A regional distribution manager for packaged plastics was planning for the expansion of a central warehouse to meet growing requirements. Before making his investment decision, he assigned an analyst to review the needs of three new products that were also candidates for the warehouse.

The analyst reported that each business needed to know how its information system needs would be affected before the businesses could decide whether to move products to the warehouse. The manager feared months of delay because information systems planning can be a lengthy process, especially if the needs of three product groups had to be considered. Such a delay would require him to lease other space at high rates and risk service quality disruption.

Stakeholders

There were four types of stakeholders.

- The three product managers wanted their products to be available in a timely way in the right locations. They each used different order, inventory, and delivery information systems and didn't want their customer service people to have to change just to accommodate somebody else.

- The three business information systems managers needed to understand the options to properly evaluate them.

- The warehousing specialists needed to understand the products' requirements and decide if they could meet them at reasonable cost.

- The warehouse operator had a stake in having a single computer system, or at least operationally identical systems, to avoid problems with his own personnel at the warehouse.

Role of Visual Language

A visual language mapping workshop was employed because the distribution manager needed a consensus plan in a short period of time. He scheduled a one-and-a-half-day session for the 15 key people with the objectives of

- Developing a shared understanding of the requirements of each business

- Identifying any conflicts

- Constructing a broad technical architecture to meet the overall needs

- Developing an action plan to migrate operations to the new warehouse

Results/Benefits

Mapping helped each business make clear how it wanted to operate and showed the similarities and differences with the three products. The majority of needs were common and the collaborative spirit of the workshop helped find ways to satisfy the differences. The action planning surfaced internal and resource obstacles that the regional manager was able to help with, and the need to acquire temporary space was avoided. The warehouse design was finalized quickly and the project went forward.

A complete and fully documented information systems plan was developed from the workshop decisions within three weeks and serves as a guide for the distribution systems for all products in the region. The mutual understanding gained during the workshop eventually led to the three products fully sharing new information systems and other elements of product management.

A valuable additional result of the workshop was to shake the paradigm that information systems planning need always be a lengthy exercise. While such efforts normally involve teams of specialists who interview business people and then draw conclusions, this distribution/warehousing example brought the systems and business stakeholders together for a brief, intense session. In a day and a half they mapped out how they wanted the process to work and what information was needed and then they built a plan together. The full plan was detailed in weeks, rather than months.

Besides meeting the distribution manager's specific objective, the stakeholders learned from each other and developed an appreciation for each other's perspectives that helped them in later projects.

SUMMARY

In each of these examples, groups of stakeholders came together and solved problems, but at the same time they built interworking skills and bonds. They addressed their tasks very efficiently but also increased their personal effectiveness and contributed small, successful steps toward organization renewal. By showing that the process of getting things done can sometimes be easy and energizing, they set expectations for better organization performance in other areas and created the demand for new rhythm on a broader scale.

FINDING A STARTING POINT

This chapter aims to give the reader a sample of possible starting points for using visual language. This is a breakthrough technology, but it will do you no good if you store the information away on a bookshelf because you can't find a place to try it.

BENEFITS TO LOOK FOR

Before addressing how you might start using visual languages, here is a summary of some of the ways visual languages can bring benefits.

1. Improve your personal effectiveness through
   a. Access to your emotional resources as well as your intellectual resources
   b. Increased creativity
   c. Better communication

2. Improve your group's or process's effectiveness through

    a. Increased interworking skills and bonding

    b. Greater group thinking and problem-solving capability

    c. Time efficiency

3. Renew your organization through

    a. Speed of group decision making

    b. An effective rhythm of participative leadership

    c. Increased enthusiasm and entrepreneurial spirit

Bring these benefits back to mind if you start to fret about where to begin!

RESISTANCE TO THE VISUAL APPROACH

If you have been schooled in scientific disciplines and respect only hard data and facts, you may remain skeptical about the value of emotion, intuition, and right-brain synthesis. You may think that the cartoonlike symbols you've seen in this book are a gimmick and an excuse to play at the office. You may feel that visual language has merit but that such a lightweight approach to problems would not be taken seriously in your company. You may think that you would be scorned for even suggesting a visual language approach to problem solving. If you don't have nagging feelings similar to these, certainly many of your colleagues do.

Visual tools differ from conventional tools because the tasks they address (generating creative thinking and channeling human energy) are different from conventional tasks. This may sound logical to you but may not change your mind. As you've read in this book, intellectual arguments alone seldom have much impact on emotional issues. If you are not convinced of their value by now, the only way to get excited about them is by using them.

One senior executive, after sponsoring and participating in an intense visual language workshop, said, "I have to admit that I didn't believe this approach would work. Visual language seemed frivolous when I first heard about it and I thought it would be a waste of time. I only agreed in the end because a number of my people wanted to try using it. I'll always be a numbers man, but I've seen that pictures really do have a place. They helped shed light on our situation, helped us discuss the undiscussable, and helped pull the group together. We wouldn't have solved these problems without visual language."

Experience is the best teacher and, given the opportunity, visual language will prove its power. Comments like "I didn't take it seriously until I started seeing the whole problem right in front of my eyes" are not unusual. Often, it is the converted skeptic who goes on to preach the value of an uninhibited atmosphere and the neutral, visual communication medium that keeps the central problem directly in front at all times.

SELECTING AN ISSUE TO ADDRESS

If one of the examples in the earlier chapters caught your attention and you foresee benefits from a similar workshop in your company, you are ready to go on to consider what language you will use. If not, the following paragraphs give you some further guidance on how to find high payback opportunities.

An issue is a good one for a visual language workshop if

- It relates to a process or strategy
- It is complex and involves several groups
- The stakeholders have energy to solve it

Areas where you will likely find such conditions and potential benefits include

- Where organization missions are not clear
- Where continuous quality improvement programs need an infusion of energy, creativity, and teamwork
- Where multicultural teams need a mechanism to improve their communication and help them think better together as a group
- Functional areas where cross-functional communication needs are particularly strong and organization restructuring is frequent, including supply chain, customer service, sales and marketing, information systems, and administration
- When planning organization changes

The following paragraphs address these points in detail.

Area 1. Mission Statements

As the knowledge content of jobs has risen, the need for a clearly shared purpose has become more acute. During the 1960s and 1970s, many companies tried to address this with programs promoting mission statements, position charters, and measures of performance, and in the 1980s there were similar programs for writing vision statements. These programs had the right idea but did not live up to their promise, partly because they were not driven to the business process level and partly because they were strictly top down and not participative. They resulted in high-level, vague, idealistic statements that were not brought to a point where they wre actionable. When you don't contribute to your mission statement,you are probably not motivated by it, and if you can't see yourself in your organization's vision, it won't guide you in your work.

If your objective is to build shared purpose and unlock the energy and commitment found only in ownership, start by making sure that each individual understands how he or she fits in the organization and asking each to contribute his or her ideas for improvement. The overall mission or vision of the enterprise starts at the top, but it must be refined at the process level, where the main work of the organization is done, and become the product of every stakeholder in each major process. Holding workshops for staff members at all levels of the company can harmonize processes and raise vitality to higher levels.

Area 2. Continuous Quality Improvement Programs

The second area where visual language could help is total quality management programs. Most quality tools are highly analytic. While there are good reasons and uses for statistical measurement and quantitative tools, visual tools can have immediate and important benefits to the human component of quality. Intuition and creativity can be highly useful in performing opportunity audits of work processes. An opportunity audit is a quick review of a process that relies on the intuition of the stakeholders to identify weak spots to be solved. Process maps built with visual languages are an efficient method for this and also can be used to develop a concept for redesign.

Continuous improvement relies on the stimulation one person gives to another. Just as many great discoveries in physics in this century have come from focused conversations among scientists, process improvements require the stimulation of focused discussion. When visual maps are built to show the wholeness of a process and its interrelationship with its environment, this stimulation occurs on both an intellectual and emotional level. Fortuitous by-products are the bonding of stakeholders and commitment to implement the ideas.

Area 3. Multicultural Teams

As companies strive to become both more diverse at home and more global in their outlook, cross-cultural communication problems will increase. The fact that personal prisons are more obvious when nationalities, skin colors, and languages are different does not make the communication task easier. Visual methods are very stimulating to openness. When everyone in a group is forced to use a language other than his or her own, it levels the communication playing field, reduces the likelihood of domination by one using his or her native tongue, and helps general understanding by requiring that all points be put into the context of a map or image. The symbols increase precision of communication because, even though there is some risk of culturally different interpretations of symbols, their visual nature stimulates discussion about them and the context of the language's metaphor serves as a reasonability check.

Area 4. Functional Areas

With hierarchies now flatter and cross-functional communication needs higher, stakeholders have to manage their processes as teams. Processes with a high number of stakeholders in different geographic areas and disciplines can particularly benefit from visual language. The following functions, where visual tools have already proven valuable, may serve as a starting point.

Supply Chain

The supply chain, all of the operations from ordering raw ingredients through delivery of finished products, is an excellent candidate for process redesign and a good place to use visual symbol languages because

- The supply chain is a complex process, typically involving from six to 10 functions, where group efficiency is a critical success factor.

- Bringing pieces of knowledge together into a manageable whole is greatly facilitated by a visual language.

- Symbols level the communication playing field. No one can speak in insider's jargon when using visual symbols.

- The playful nature of the medium excites intuition and generates a level of group creativity that may have been ground down in the daily struggle to get products to customers.

Supply chain workshops, which may include customers or suppliers, yield both short- and long-term benefits, most often including

- Improved scheduling, order entry process simplification, better inquiry handling, lower cost of quality, inventory reduction, and lower total costs

- Better customer service and on-time delivery

- Lower human resource requirements, fewer turf issues, higher team spirit, and personal commitment to results

A recent workshop held in Singapore is a good example of both a supply chain problem and a multicultural team. Fifteen people came together from nine countries in North and South America, Europe, Australia, and Asia to plan how the start-up of a new manufacturing plant should change the distribution pattern of raw materials and finished products in the region and in the world. Each person knew a piece of the whole, but a solid plan required everyone's combined knowledge. Most of the people had never met each other and they were separated by native cultures, languages, and professional disciplines. Even though the group members had all these prisons to contend with, by using a visual language they were able to deal with the complex issues before them and build a comprehensive plan in only two days. By the end of the session, they were starting to feel and act like a team!

Sales and Marketing

Sales and marketing people seem to have an affinity for visual languages. They are avid map builders, in direct proportion to their distaste for long analyses and thick written documents. They like the interactive personal contact of group sessions that provide a fertile environment for

- Discussing the processes and forces at work in markets and customers' companies
- Raising and resolving strongly held, opposing ideas in a friendly, satisfying way
- Resolving complex issues in a short time
- Generating team spirit and intense personal commitment

Customer Service

High-quality customer service usually requires excellent access to company information and excellent coordination of a number of functions that are not hierarchically related.

Making continuous, sustainable quality improvements requires involvement and commitment from a wide and sometimes antagonistic group of stakeholders. Visual language workshops can be particularly useful to customer service groups because

- They help individuals see the big picture and how they fit in.
- Their speed means that supervisors and representatives can jointly solve problems without spending long periods of time away from their day-to-day responsibilities.

Customer service workshops often result in

- A realization that virtually every function in a company should play a role in customer service
- Better mutual understanding, cooperation, and teamwork
- Identification of measurement points to control quality
- Well-defined projects to improve information flow
- Higher status for the customer service function

Information Systems

Planning for information systems is a challenging task because

- It often involves a wide number of business functions and groups with differing priorities and uses for different information.
- A two-culture problem between technically oriented systems people and market-oriented business people can hinder communication, stifle fresh ideas, and leave lingering animosity.

Visual languages level the communication playing field, allowing the diversity of views to stimulate creativity rather than create barriers. The single set of jointly created visual images that results from the workshop works to keep the group united in its purpose and to focus its energy on achieving results. These images or maps usually can be translated quite easily into the flow diagrams loved by information systems professionals.

Information systems plans developed with visual languages are characterized by

- Creative and practical solutions
- Mutual understanding between systems users and service providers
- Higher end-user ownership of the plan

Administration

Public administration groups often operate with the liability that their objectives and measures of performance are not precise. In international service organizations, they may be high-minded, vague, and subject to differing interpretations. Administration groups in businesses are generally quite far removed from customers and the sense of purpose and energy that customer contact can bring. These factors can rob administrative functions of their energy, sap their interest in quality, and allow small matters to stay under active or passive dispute for long periods of time.

Visual language can be particularly effective here because

- Building maps demands that objectives and processes be made clear and provides a tool where this can be done intuitively and quickly.

- Mapping requires that customers and other stakeholders constantly be evident when showing administrative processes, focusing discussions, and sharpening objectives and measures.

- Showing obstacles through symbols helps the group identify problems rooted in the organization culture or environment.

The benefits that result from administration workshops regularly include

- Quality improvement

- Cost reduction

- Better focus on customers

- Teamwork and commitment to consensus objectives

Area 5. Organization Changes

The task of defining or redefining an organization's structure can put a manager and staff under a great deal of pressure. The task requires a balancing of several conflicting issues.

- Personal leadership duties

- The need for participation

- The need to avoid prolonged uncertainty

- Special interests of personnel

- Pressure of business requirements

These conflicting forces can combine to make the ideal solution elusive. A visual language workshop can help because

- It grounds the leadership group in a common view of today's operation and its weaknesses.

- It lets the group members explore alternatives, based on how acting on stated values could change operational processes or how different assumptions about the environment could impact them.

- A map of how the organization's processes ideally will work is a clear guide to how the organization should be structured.

- Additional visual language workshops can include more people at lower levels to refine and detail the envisioned processes after the leadership group has set direction about the overall structure.

This approach can help achieve

1. Wide and constructive involvement of organization members

   a. All staff members have the opportunity to contribute fully at an appropriate time. Maps let them contribute their ideas and test them with their peers and managers in a nonthreatening way.

   b. The focus of the group is on building the future, not on defending today's personal turf.

2. Better structures and plans

   a. Maps keep structure considerations within context of the organization's objectives, processes, and values.

   b. Visual language workshops bring out the most creative and practical ideas your organizations can develop.

   c. Visual plans encourage identification of quality measures and considerations of risks, obstacles, and help needed.

3. Efficiency

   a. Visual language workshops shorten the time needed to think through organization structure decisions.

   b. The new organization will reach a high level of effectiveness in a short time because the high level of participation in the design increases commitment.

SELECT A VISUAL METHOD

You have at least three options on how to start with visual languages. One way is to not use a language at all but to experiment with visual imagery by making a drawing of your issue. This may sound simple but can be quite complex because, unless you intend to make a straightforward representation of the subject matter, you have to decide on a metaphor and then draw the symbols. This approach could, however, be an act of discovery because the image or picture you draw may evolve and grow to become a full language.

If you have a specialized need, you may set out to create your own new language. This is an ambitious route to take if you have no experience with visual languages and will take considerable preparation. Guidance on how to build a visual language is presented in the appendix.

If you want to start by building a map of your issue with symbols like those found in this book, you can acquire color booklets of them from the Visual Language Research Center.[1] You could augment those symbols by cutting out or drawing images that may be unique to your organization or function.

When you've decided on the issue you want to address, selected a visual method, and reviewed chapter 6, you are ready to plan your workshop and get started!

SUMMARY AND CONCLUSION

"Communication = words" is one of the most firmly entrenched paradigms we hold but, for communication among different disciplines and cultures, visual languages provide an additional channel for information exchange and verification that makes them more effective than strictly verbal languages. When issues are complex, visual language provides a highly disciplined thinking method that facilitates systematic group thinking and consideration of process, environment, and values. When innovation and teamwork are needed, visual languages provide stimulation and idea representation methods that verbal languages cannot. Intensively employing your visual sense lets you draw on your right-brain functionality and emotional resources as well as your left-brain analytical capability and helps you make your problems mind-sized.

This book has described many examples of how visual languages have been used successfully, has explained the underlying reasons for visual language's power, and has shown you how and when to use visual languages. There are no doubt many new uses yet to be tried and benefits gained.

The playful appearance of visual language may be an obstacle to your trying it, but take caution from a newly coined proverb: "Don't let a beaver dam block your progress." Try visual languages. You have little to lose and a lot to gain!

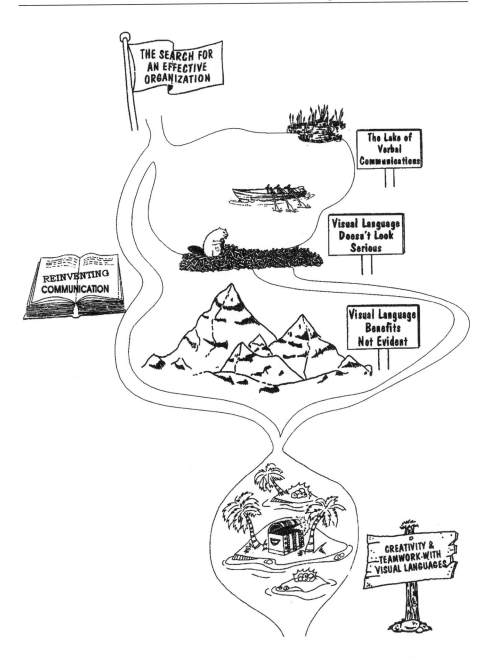

Figure 8.1

HOW TO BUILD
A VISUAL LANGUAGE

This final section is primarily for the adventuresome who are convinced of the concept of visual languages and are ready to take the plunge and invest the effort to build one. It will also be of interest to those who want to deepen their understanding of why they are so effective.

WHY BUILD A VISUAL LANGUAGE?

You are most likely to build your own language if you foresee a special payback. The starting point is, of course, having an objective that can be fulfilled by a custom-made language. When setting objectives, you need to be in close touch with your organization's underlying philosophy and know where its leadership wants it to go. The vocabulary, technology, and accompanying communication process give you, the designer, many mechanisms to meet your objectives.

Most organizations have a clear identity and some of their own unique jargon. A language may aim to deepen the capabilities of the group and complement and add to its jargon. This may make the group more exclusive. On the other hand, the language may aim to open up the group to be more inclusive of others by making its existing jargon more accessible.

A language can serve specific tasks and it can also help establish a community. It emerges from a culture, shapes it, and is in turn shaped by the evolution of that culture. It can establish paradigms that help focus an organization and define what is important, similar to the way the front page of a newspaper shapes a community's discussions and priorities.

Visual language can be a valuable tool for leaders who need to set direction in a participative manner because it has the potent asset of being able to access emotional resources. A leader who wants true change needs to address values and turn them into actions, a task for which the visual medium is well suited.

LANGUAGE APPLICATIONS

It is important that you don't let the examples of visual language shown earlier in the book limit your thinking about the nature and potential uses of visual languages. Languages could be developed to address the needs of specific functions or companies or activities common to many functions or companies. Some possibilities are

A. Planning tools

   1. End result objective setting

   2. Process redesign

      a. Stakeholder analysis

      b. SWOT analysis (strengths, weaknesses, opportunities, threats)

      c. Process analysis

      d. Process visioning

B. Leading tools

   1. Strategy setting

   2. Action planning

   3. Improvement opportunity audit

C. Organizing tools

    1. Mapping organization onto business processes

    2. Defining roles and relationships

D. People management tools

    1. Performance management

        a. Establishing points of measurement

        b. Objective setting

        c. Performance review

    2. Delegation

E. Skill building

    1. Thinking skills

    2. Creativity skills

    3. Innovation process

    4. Time management

    5. Problem solving with enhanced fishbone diagrams

    6. Root cause analysis

F. Personal development

    1. Career planning

    2. Life planning

    3. Family problem solving

    4. Mental health problem identification

G. Customer satisfaction surveys

H. Customer needs analysis

I. Negotiation

J. Performance characterization and control

This list is not intended to be exhaustive but rather to show some of the many domains where new tools could be useful. If you see some area here or are thinking of another where a visual language would be useful, you should try to state clearly your objective for it. You should consider both the specific application and the overall culture within which it would function. You should investigate whether a suitable language is available and cost-effective when compared to the costs and benefits of a custom-tailored language for your situation.

METAPHORS

The primary challenge is to find a metaphor to drive the selection of symbols and provide the unifying theme that will serve as the language's syntax. The metaphor provides the storyboard background and must fit the dimensions of the task.

If your objective is quite limited, such as developing a means of stimulating thinking about how to supply goods to customers at minimum cost, your language might consist solely of the following drawing.

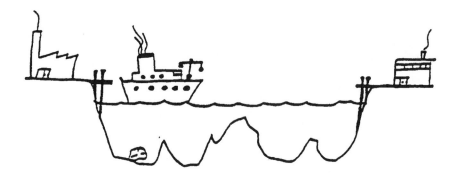

You could define your vocabulary as follows:

- The factory on the left represents the supplier.
- The factory at the right is the customer.
- The ship is the means of transport.
- Rocks are obstacles to timely delivery.
- The water is extra inventory to make sure the ship can get to the customer with no problems.

When you first define the symbols to a group of supply chain managers, you are explaining your view that inventory is a means of buying protection from problems such as the inability to accurately forecast demand. You could go on to use the drawing to provoke their thinking about ways to improve efficiency. You could assert that there are an unlimited number of improvements that can be made in the supply chain and ask participants to look at the drawing and think of how they could achieve them.

By comparing the inventory problem to this picture, you are asking the supply chain managers to see the problem in a different way and may be opening up new avenues of thought. For example, they may identify some of the rocks on the seabed and suggest how they could eliminate or reduce them. They could improve performance by making the ship go faster. They could make the cargo lighter and lower the waterline of the ship. They could use an airplane rather than a ship. They could build a bridge and use a truck. They could build a tunnel. They could build a small plant right on the customer's site, and so forth.

If your objective is a language to convey feelings or perceptions at a given moment, your metaphor could be simple and direct, such as characterizing your feelings about yourself or others by using symbols of animals. The individual's interpretation of the symbol is the starting point for communicating about feelings caused by the situation.[1] The metaphor can be extended by showing cages, environmental constraints, or predators.

If the task is yet more complex and needs to show resulting action, the animal can be shown in its current context, but with optional actions, such as climbing a tree, diving into a hole in the ground, fighting defensively, or attacking. Alternatives, multiple protagonists, generations of protagonists, help providers, time lapses, sequences, or other dimensions all could be represented by symbols if the metaphor is sufficiently broad.

Each metaphor provides varying richness of optional symbols. More dimensions and richness would make the tool more complicated to teach and use but too few options may leave a tool inadequate for a task.

A visual metaphor helps people find a way to express complex circumstances and emotions and helps others understand more clearly. Spontaneous metaphors, as created in free-form drawing, can take many forms and perhaps fit the circumstance perfectly. If the drawing is not of a familiar metaphor, however, its full meaning will be limited to those present at the creation. A predesigned, familiar metaphor, on the other hand, provides a structure that satisfies our need for rationality and logic. It provides a shorthand, ready-made set of characteristics and relationships from which we can divine a whole when seeing only a part.

A metaphor is a model used to communicate and understand a situation. The one you chose ideally will put the group in the frame of mind where the symbols employed evoke interest, energy, and connectedness to the issue at hand. People of different cultures and the different sexes will develop more or less interest and energy for different metaphors depending on their personal experience with the metaphor.

The following list gives an idea of the numerous potential metaphors that might be appropriate for different objectives.

Nature metaphors

- Animals
- The continents
- Islands
- Ocean currents

- Rivers
- Caves
- Gardens growing
- Trees
- Ecosystems
- Air currents
- Clouds, weather
- Seasons
- Day/night

Human experience metaphors

- Sports
- Mountain climbing
- Digging tunnels
- Safari
- Desert trek
- Space voyage
- Searching for gold
- Chase
- Fables, myths
- Religious stories
- Historical events
- Mystery
- Book or movie themes
- Movie making
- House building, interior design
- Food gathering or preparation
- Heroic adventures: medieval knights, samurai, and so on
- War, different historical eras
- Breaking out of jail
- Navigating a ship
- Flying an aircraft
- Driving on a highway
- Time travel

- Music, recording
- Occupations: work of a surgeon, mail carrier, programmer
- Games or gambling: chess, capture the flag, cards
- Political and government processes

Physical metaphors

- Human body
- Life cycle
- Cities
- Train systems

How-it-is-done metaphors

- Farming
- Fishing
- Newspaper publishing
- Building a factory

You can combine metaphors or nest them to achieve an objective. The use of a map as a background metaphor is an example. As you saw in both the river mapping and village mapping examples, the metaphor of a map supports the primary metaphors that relate a river journey to a strategy and a village to a business process. Maps are helpful in visual languages because nearly everybody has had experience in using a map and understands how it relates to real terrain. The concepts of scale and scope are inherent in maps and most people have an innate sense of what they imply and are able to move up or down a level of detail without becoming disoriented.

When selecting a metaphor, you as the tool builder have to consider the dimensions of the task you are trying to facilitate, such as

- An inner, personal state of being or emotion
- A snapshot of a dynamic state of a process
- Movement through time
- Multiple time periods juxtaposed with each other
- Alternatives and decisions
- Other dimensions

Your choice of metaphor influences what symbols you will use, but the availability of suitable symbols also can influence your choice. The final test is an intuitive, emotional one. Does the overall theme or gestalt of the metaphor fit with your objectives?

SYMBOLS

The type of symbols you choose will follow from your objectives.
Some classes of symbols include

- Objectives
- Alternatives and decisions
- Actions, events, obstacles, and risks
- Organization structures and functions
- Communication of information
- Qualitative indicators
- Roles, responsibilities, and behaviors

If you intend your language to serve community objectives as well as a functional objective, the metaphor will need symbols to show

- Values, beliefs, guidelines, and standards
- Economic, competitive, human, or other environmental factors

While a pervasive, unifying metaphor is probably a prerequisite for coherency in a language with many symbols, it is possible to build a simple language with no metaphor. For example, a small visual language called *leadership conduct contracting* was developed to be used when a manager and staff are named for a new project. Its intent is to ensure an appropriate level of discussion and a clear understanding of roles and expected behaviors. Aimed primarily at the project manager, it uses only four behavior symbols to discuss the range of possibilities and to determine an appropriate style.

This symbol shows people talking. This type of informal discussion may be expected when the merits of a project are not yet formally decided and input is needed from a variety of internal people or customers. A key skill to be applied at this stage is listening.

This list of names on a scroll is intended to show enrollment of an expedition, where people and other resources are organized. This type of activity occurs only after a decision has been made to proceed. Convincing and selling are needed skills.

This finger pointing the way on a map indicates leadership while a project is underway. The balance of participative versus authoritarian style should be discussed.

The steamroller indicates a responsibility to take strong, independent action to overcome any obstacles. If this symbol is chosen as the agreed leadership style, it represents a risk in itself and requires an extra degree of monitoring by senior management.

Open discussion, agreement, and communication to others about the expected style of leadership are the objectives of this small language. It doesn't try to cover all aspects of conduct but only aspires to ensure that the subjects of roles, responsibilities, and behaviors are fully discussed. Because of its simplicity, the language succeeds without a metaphor.

QUALITIES OF SYMBOLS

Symbols should be chosen to keep the core of the language simple and functional. An ideal symbol is one that fits the metaphor, is immediately recognizable to everyone in the community, and does not have to be explained. It represents its subject accurately and carries an emotional message at the same time.

The metaphor provides the syntax and grammar within which the symbol delivers its meaning. If the metaphor is a river, the water flows downhill and activities occur in time sequence along the bank. If it is a sport, the natural sequence of the game and rules apply.

Symbols should be consistent with the metaphor, but some liberty can be taken to meet the tool's objectives. As long as no violent conflict is created, the tool builder can engage the observer's imagination in order to employ an image that best represents its intended purpose. Clarity before purity!

Symbols can be drawn faithfully or in caricature. They may or may not include elements of humor depending on the overall tone sought. Take care that too much humor doesn't detract from the symbol's message.

Color is critical to attracting attention, giving life, and imparting emotional messages. Color symbolism may be employed and the overall appearance of a completed map or image, including the background color, should suit both the metaphor and mood of the exercise. The fact that this book's examples are not in color should not make you think that color is optional. You don't get much emotional reaction to a black and white fire!

When possible, symbols themselves should not contain any writing for two reasons: to reduce intrusions of left-brain sequential thinking into the map-building process and to maintain verbal/written language independence. Identifiers, such as signposts, can be employed to allow users to give specific meaning to symbols where needed. On a crowded map, however, it may be necessary to integrate labels into the symbols.

If you develop a language with many symbols, you may need to provide a dictionary of images for users. The dictionary may describe a symbol's fixed meaning or its generic meaning, allowing the user to modify and interpret it to her own situation. You can choose not to provide a dictionary when you want users to spend time thinking about the symbols and perhaps developing different interpretations of them.

TECHNOLOGIES

The technology underlying a visual symbol language determines how one physically creates symbols and lets users arrange them to convey their messages.

Of the many materials available, paper has the advantages of being lightweight, easy to find, and inexpensive. This would also apply to the background surface which needs to be large enough for clear presentation but of a manageable size, between 2 feet by 2 feet and 4 feet by 4 feet. Tools generally require moveable symbols so that users can change their minds and reposition symbols. For this, removable adhesive can be applied to the background surface or to the symbols themselves. After an image or map is completed, it is generally impractical to reuse paper symbols at other sessions.

Symbols can be drawn by pencil or pen, drawn by computer software, or created photographically. They can be reproduced with a color photocopier. They could be cut out from plain paper and applied to an adhesive background surface. They could be photocopied onto precut self-adhesive labels and applied to a plain background surface. Four-color printing and die cutters specially shaped for the images are best when high volume and highest quality are required, but would incur a much higher cost.

Magnets and magnetic boards are an alternative means of sticking symbols to a surface and allowing them to be reused, but there are drawbacks, including magnets blocking the symbols and the need to rewrite identifiers.

Transparent overlay background sheets can be used to build layers onto a model, showing either additional complexity or changes in time.

Completed models may be photographed and photocopied, scanned into a computer, or rebuilt on a computer using a library of previously scanned symbols.

The visual languages described in this book have been two dimensional. Three-dimensional objects offer the opportunity to build board-game-type tools and to make highly detailed images which may be appropriate or necessary for some uses. They have the disadvantages of being more complex to design, costly to make, and more difficult to capture and store in an end-result image, but this could be overcome if the need justified it.

A computer-based medium offers advantages for creating or tailoring symbols, expanding the size of a vocabulary, facilitating the building, and changing the maps. The possible addition of animation or sounds to symbols could give them added interest and usefulness. Storing final images, layering text explanations under the symbols, and printing out end-product images and stories also make computer technology a very interesting potential base technology for a tool.

The computer is a valuable symbol development aid, but at this writing there are some drawbacks to its use as a workshop vehicle. Large-scale screens that three to six people can work around are not yet offered at moderate price. The technology for selecting and placing symbols is oriented toward a workstation with a keyboard or mouse and tends to bring the left brain back into dominance. Touch selection and placement would circumvent this problem and open up new uses of computer power.

The ultimate technology for a visual language is probably projection of holograms summoned by use of spoken words or thoughts, but this will probably have to wait for the next century.

GROUP PROCESSES

As you design the group processes for your new language you need to be clear about your objectives. The guidance in this section assumes that your primary objective will be to achieve a superior level of communication and creativity in a subject area. It also assumes that you want a high level of active involvement by all participants and a balance between comfort and challenge.

There are two subobjectives you should consider: building interworking skills and building emotional bonds among participants. Interworking is a part of teamwork. It is the skill of working together with other people on shared tasks. It is developed through doing. If interworking skill improvement is your objective, your visual language and image-building process ideally should provide for many joint tasks that include physical movement such as passing materials and other small services. Repetition forms habits and interworking relationships on a motor level that encourage the same on an intellectual level in the map or image-building activity. When you build interworking skills, you collect information about the needs of your collaborators, you learn rules they follow and signals they give, and how your own actions can complement or detract from theirs. Interworking is usually enhanced by positive emotions between the parties, but it can exist without them.

If you want your language to build effective communities, you need more than good communication and interworking skill, you need community members to feel bonded. Bonding is a feeling of unity with others in a group that results from intense emotions during shared experiences. Bonding is different from interworking because it is an emotion rather than a skill. It does, however, exist in many teams with good interworking skills and participants can help it to occur faster and be deepened if they are part of the shared emotional experience.

Bonding is characterized by a sense of belonging and comradeship. It is sustained by public recognition of the uniqueness of the group and reminiscing about the bonding experience. After an emotional experience, group members want to display their identity. "I climbed Pikes Peak" T-shirts are bought not to celebrate a victory over the mountain but to signal bonding with an "elite" community. The same goes in many cases for baseball caps, commemorative rings, and plaques. When you design your visual language processes, you have the opportunity to structure communication sessions so that they encourage bonding.

Shared jeopardy situations are opportunities to create bonding.[2] Often used in initiation rites, they draw from three emotions: fear, salvation, and satisfaction.

You share jeopardy when you climb a mountain cliff with others attached to your rope. You share jeopardy whenever you and your group are at risk and will succeed or fail together, whether because of each other's efforts or because of forces beyond your control. Fear of failure, even a small one and even if felt for only a brief period, breaks down smugness and arrogance and makes most people seek the security of a group identity. In this frame of mind, people are generally more interested to communicate their needs, more keen to understand the needs of others, and more willing to share their knowledge for the common good.

Shared jeopardy can be a useful part of a visual language communication process. The question is how to give people a small degree of insecurity and the subsequent experiences of salvation and satisfaction. Running the rapids of the Colorado in a raft is one way, but it is probably more practical and productive to stay in the office, maintain focus on the problem at hand, and simply raise the bar on your issue. You can set high objectives for small groups, implicitly put them in competition with each other, and provide only brief training in how to use their tools (just a few words on how to do the breast stroke before throwing them into the pool).

You can start your visual communication session by assigning the group a task after only a brief introduction to the language. Warning that each person is a candidate to present his or her subgroup's completed image within an hour generates an unspoken but palpable anxiety in each participant. ("Not only am I being asked to use a new language, but I have to represent a very complex situation that I don't completely understand in a very short time.") As individuals look across the room at what their colleagues are doing, they deepen their fear that they are inadequate for the task: "Everyone else seems to be making more progress than we are."

When a subgroup colleague has an idea of where to start and places the first symbol on the background sheet, there is both a burst of admiration for him or her and a feeling of salvation that comes over the members. Each subsequent exercise holds a degree of these emotions, but the first experience is the most intense. For that reason, workshop designers try to assign to the same first subgroup those people who, for one reason or another, need to be brought closer together.

Satisfaction is experienced when the subgroup members complete their first image or map. The sense of accomplishment and ownership is very high and they have their "T-shirt," a shared creation on the wall showing their combined knowledge and insights that their colleagues can appreciate.

The supportive behaviors among members within a bonded community represent the best we can hope for in organizations. The community bond may erode over time if members have few interactions, but its existence may still leave behind some important individual member-to-member bonds that take on new life. When the community remains active, new shared history strengthens the bond and provides a way for new members to enter.

An ideal workshop process is one that feels completely natural because it flows smoothly and allows easy interaction among people. If serious work can be made to seem like play, creativity is promoted. Creative thinking is largely metaphorical, and in play everything is metaphorical. If you are building a sand castle and imagining it to be real, you're using a metaphor. If you play with baseball cards or dolls, it is metaphorical. Any provocation for using a metaphor, however marginally appropriate, helps you to see the situation in new ways.

Using symbols to send messages sometimes can work wonders. For example, a visual map of a plan to implement a new business process was being presented to a group to build support for the project. One of the rivers was blocked by a fallen tree that was labeled "entrenched, old manufacturing systems." One plant computer manager in the audience who had been negative toward the project focused on the fallen tree and assumed (rightly) that it was meant to represent her and her group. This characterization was visibly upsetting to her. She turned red, moved around in her seat, shook her head, and made several references to not being a blocker. Over the coming weeks she became very active to prove how helpful she and her group could be and how that symbol should not apply to her.

Play also promotes bonding. Play recalls a state of innocence and a time of real openness between friends. Although everyone, when he or she was young, experienced hurt and meanness on the playground, friends had little to hide and were valued for who they were and not for their rank. Play tends to clear away obstructions to fully sharing bonding emotions when they may arise. After one or two visual language communication sessions, a group becomes familiar with the symbols and techniques. In subsequent sessions, visual languages themselves contribute less to shared jeopardy and any jeopardy must come mostly from the challenge of the problem being considered. Constructive play then becomes more important and the shared pleasure of it replaces fear as the lubricating emotion for the effectiveness of the session and as nourishment for the group's bond.

Visual language sessions typically end with everyone in high spirits if not elated with their accomplishments. Photographs or copies of the images or maps built by the group make excellent "T-shirts" because they are novel, are attention getting, and speak directly about the task at hand.

If the language and process have been fully successful, all participants will be able to see themselves in each of the maps. They will be able to see how they fit in the structure today, understand what they will do differently, and know what actions they have to take to get there. The map copies that group members display on their desks remind them of their shared history and shared commitments. The images they keep in their memories act as an internal compass to help them move forward in harmony.

REFERENCE NOTES

Preface

1. Anne Hope and Sally Timmel, *Training for Transformation, A Handbook for Community Workers* (Gweru, Zimbabwe: Mambo Press, 1984). This three-volume series contains a variety of visual tools used for training in Africa.

   The following book also shows visual tools and participatory techniques used in developing countries. Lyra Srinivasan, *Tools for Community Participation* (New York: PROWWESS/UNDP, 1990).

Chapter 3

1. Otto Kroeger and Janet M. Thuesen, *Type Talk* (New York: Dell Publishing, 1988), 6–22. Kroeger and Thuesen explain how the the Meyers-Briggs Type Indicator™ builds 16 personality types based on how you interact with the world (are you an introvert or reserved toward other people, or are you an extrovert or outgoing with others?); how you gather data (are you a sensor, preferring precise and tangible data, or are you intuitive, preferring general and interrelated data?); how you make decisions (are you a thinker, being objective, firm, and clear, or are you a feeler, empathizing and accommodating?); your life orientation (are you a judger, highly ordered with strong opinions, or are you a perceiver, spontaneous and with open options?).

   More information can be found in David Keirsy and Marilyn Bates, *Please Understand Me* (Del Mar, Calif.: Gnosology Books, 1984).

2. John R. Johnson, "Understanding Misunderstanding: A Key to Effective Communication," *Training and Development Journal* (August 1983): 62–68.

3. John Greenleaf Whittier, "Maud Muller," *The Poetical Works of Whittier*, Hyatt H. Waggoner, ed. (Boston: Houghton Mifflin, 1975), 47.

Chapter 4

1. Robert Ornstein and Paul Ehrlich, *New World New Mind* (New York: Doubleday, 1989), 37–39.

2. Sharon Begley, "The Flintstone Diagnosis," *Newsweek* (May 10, 1993), 62–63.

3. Max Lüscher, *The Lüscher Color Test* (New York: Random House, 1969), 9–16.

4. A number of books have referred to and drawn conclusions from the work of Roger Sperry and others about brain hemisphere specialization, including

Betty Edwards, *Drawing on the Artist Within* (New York: Simon & Schuster, 1986), 10–12.

Peter Russell, *The Brain Book* (London: Routledge & Kegan Paul, 1979), 48–63.

Tony Buzan, *Make the Most of Your Mind* (London: Colt Books, 1977), 10–16.

5. Ned Herrmann, *The Creative Brain* (Lake Lure, N.C.: Brain Books, 1988), 348.

6. For discussion of the value of intuition in business, see Weston H. Agor, "Intuition & Strategic Planning," *The Futurist* (November–December 1989), 20–23.

7. Reprinted with permission from Ned Herrmann, author of *The Creative Brain*, pages 30 (for Triune brain) and 425 (for Differences in Processing Models).

  Building on both left-right research and the Triune theory, Ned Herrmann developed a whole brain theory that shows dominance in four areas. While working at General Electric he developed a testing instrument to identify preferences for each quadrant and was able to identify characteristic behaviors, styles, and preferences for each quadrant.

Whole Brain Model

	Left	**Right**
	(A)	(D)
Cortex	Upper Left	Upper Right
	(B)	(C)
Limbic	Lower Left	Lower Right

	Upper Left A	Lower Left B	Lower Right C	Upper Right D
Descriptors	logical factual critical rational analytical quantitative authoritarian mathematical	technical reader data collector conservative controlled sequential articulate dominant detailed	musical spiritual talkative symbolic emotional intuitive (regarding people) reader (personal)	creative/ innovative intuitive (regarding solutions) simultaneous synthesizer holistic artistic spatial
Skills	problem solving analytical statistical technical financial	planning supervising administrative organizational implementation	expressing ideas interpersonal writing (correspondence) teaching training	creative innovative integrative causing change conceptualizing strategic planning
Typical phrases used	"Tools" "Hardware" "Key point" "Knowing the bottom line" "Take it apart" "Break it down" "Critical analysis"	"Establishing habits" "We have always done it this way" "Law and order" "Self discipline" "By the book" "Play it safe" "Sequence"	"Team work" "The family" "Interactive" "Participatory" "Human values" "Personal growth" "Human resources" "Team development"	"Play with an idea" "The big picture" "Cutting edge" "Broad-based" "Synergistic" "Conceptual blockbusting" "Innovative"
Typical derogatory phrases (zingers) used by others	"Number cruncher" "Power hungry" "Unemotional" "Calculating" "Uncaring" "Cold fish" "Nerd"	"Picky" "Can't think for himself" "Unimaginative" "Stick-in-the-mud" "Grinds out the task"	"Bleeding heart" "Talk, talk, talk" "Touchy-feely" "A pushover" "Soft touch" "Sappy"	"Reckless" "Can't focus" "Unrealistic" "Off-the-wall" "Dreams a lot" "Undisciplined" "Head in clouds"

Herrmann's observations include

- Profiles show primary disposition but all people have capabilities in all quadrants.
- In total, profiles are quite evenly spread across the quadrants while men's tend to cluster on the upper left and women's on the lower right.
- Individuals in diagonally opposite quadrants can have significant problems relating to one another.
- Thinking and work in all quadrants is necessary for innovation and the overall success of an organization.

The whole brain theory adds further weight to the notion that today's organizations would be strengthened if they were more open to capitalize fully on different thinking styles.

This physical approach had many similarities in result to the personality-based observations of Isabel Meyers and Katheryn Briggs. After further research findings accumulated, Herrmann decided that the four-quadrant model could not be fully justified on a physical basis, although it remained accurate on a metaphoric basis.

8. Daniel Goldman, "Brain Study Explains Power of Emotions," *International Herald Tribune* (August 17, 1989). Goldman summarizes Joseph Ledoux's findings. He also quotes noted authority Michael Gazzaniga, professor of psychiatry at Dartmouth University medical school: "It may explain why so much of emotional life is hard to understand with the rational mind." He further quotes Norman Weinberger at the Center for Neurobiology of Learning and Memory at the University of California at Irvine: "It's a missing piece of the puzzle, showing that fear can be learned without the cortex being involved."

   A related paper by Ledoux is "Sensory Systems and Emotion: A Model of Affective Processing," *Integrative Psychiatry* 4 (1986): 237–243.

9. Carl Sagan and Ann Druyan, *Shadows of Forgotten Ancestors* (New York: Random House, 1992), 110.

10. Ibid., 110–111, 205–218, and see note 7, 31.

11. See note 1, 20–21. Ornstein and Ehrlich make many other observations of interest, including our sensory system restricts incoming data to a fraction of what is really available in order to prevent overload. Most often, we are impressed only by dramatic changes in

what we see. We develop a simplified caricature of reality, highlighting points of particular interest. This is highly efficient, but caricatures are useful only if they conform closely to reality. (72–75)

12. See note 4, Russell, 115.

13. A. Fuglesang, *Applied Communication* (Stockholm, Sweden: Dag Hamersjold Foundation, 1973).

14. Carl G. Jung, *Man and His Symbols* (London: Aldus Books, 1964), 3–44.

15. Rudolf Arnheim, *Visual Thinking* (Berkeley, Calif.: University of California Press, 1969), 22.

Also about frogs,

W. R. A. Muntz, "Vision in Frogs," *Scientific American* (March 1964): 111–119.

Further information on how patterns of swiftly moving objects are stored can be found in

Jane E. Brody, "Brain Yields Clues to Its Visual Maps," *New York Times* (March 23, 1993): C1.

16. Bill Moyers, *Healing and the Mind* (New York: Doubleday, 1993).

17. There are a growing number of people who argue that we should not focus on intelligence quotient (IQ) or other standardized tests of intelligence. They argue that a person has many kinds of intelligence that are important to competence and success. These include

- Logical/mathematical
- Linguistic
- Spatial
- Bodily/kinesthetic
- Interpersonal
- Intrapersonal
- Musical

See Robert J. Sternberg and Richard K. Wagner, eds., *Practical Intelligence* (Cambridge, England: Cambridge University Press, 1986), particularly Reading 8, "The Theory of Multiple Intelligences: Some Issues and Answers," Joseph M. Walters and Howard Gardner. See also Thomas Armstrong, *7 Kinds of Smart* (New York: Penguin Books, 1993).

18. See note 15, Arnheim.

    Other comments of interest include

    "human beings and animals explore and comprehend by acting and handling rather than by mere contemplation." (vii)

    "Perceptual and pictorial shapes are not only thought products but the very flesh and blood of thinking itself." (134)

    "Language is valuable for thinking, but not because we think in words. Words help in that they lend to visual imagery. The visual medium is enormously superior because it offers structural equivalents to all characteristics of objects, events, relationships." (232)

    More on the subject of simultaneous seeing and understanding can be found in

    Semir Zeki, "The Visual Image in Brain and Mind," *Scientific American* (September 1992): 68–76.

19. W. V. Davies, *Egyptian Hieroglyphs* (London: The British Museum, 1987), 14.

Chapter 5

1. By permission of the British Library (London: The British Library, 1989), 13–14.

2. "In Alchemists Notes, Clues to Modern Chemistry," *New York Times* (April 10, 1990).

3. See note 1, 34–35.

4. George L. Dorros, *A Framework for Improving Organizational Effectiveness and Capacity to Change in Uncertain Environments* (Manila: Southeast Asia Interdisciplinary Development Institute, 1983).

5. For example, Shakti Gawain, *Creative Visualization* (Mill Valley, Calif.: Whatever Publishing, 1979).

6. W. V. Davies, *Egyptian Hieroglyphs* (London: The British Museum, 1987), 48–49.

    The Rosetta stone was a slab of black rock unearthed in 1799 that bore the same inscription in hieroglyphics and two other languages. It was the key to deciphering hieroglyphics.

Chapter 6

1. For a fully developed view of planning practice, see Russell L. Ackoff, *Creating the Corporate Future* (New York: John Wiley & Sons, 1981).

2. Betty Edwards, *Drawing on the Artist Within* (New York: Simon & Schuster, 1986), 3–5.

   For other views of creativity, see Edward de Bono, *Lateral Thinking* (London: Penguin Books, 1970) and Roger von Oech, *A Whack on the Side of the Head* (Stamford, Conn.: U.S. Games Systems, 1983).

Chapter 8

1. Visual Language Research Center, 58 Salem Street, Andover, MA 01810 USA. Telephone: 508-475-3045, Fax: 508-475-3478, Internet: 71732.1711@compuserv.com

Appendix

1. Anne Hope and Sally Timmel, *Training for Transformation, A Handbook for Community Workers* (Gweru, Zimbabwe: Mambo Press, 1984), Book 2, 71–74.

2. Josh Miner, Founding Trustee of Outward Bound in the United States, interviews by author, Andover, Mass., 29 September 1993 and 2 December 1993. Miner believes that bonding most easily occurs when shared jeopardy is present. An accompanying physical experience also is valuable because any behavioral shift requires physical action.

INDEX

ABOUT THE AUTHOR

Larry Raymond is founder and director of Visual Language Research Center and is the principal consultant at Newbase International in Andover, Massachusetts.

He holds a B.A. from the University of Massachusetts and an M.B.A. from Pace University. He has worked as a computer programmer/analyst, director of information systems planning, director of business services, sales manager, marketing manager, and management consultant. In 1988, he founded Newbase S.A., a management consulting firm in Geneva, Switzerland.

Raymond's work assignments have been on six different continents for many organizations—DuPont, Hewlett-Packard, Nestlé, Sandoz, Digital Equipment, Union Carbide, Swissair, the World Bank, the World Health Organization, the United Nations International Trade Centre, the governments of several developing countries, and other customers.

He served as adjunct professor of management at Webster University in Geneva for 10 years. During that time he developed a unique perspective on the communication, planning, and problem-solving difficulties of multicultural organizations. Research and practical experience led to the development of the principles of visual language described in this book.